OVERCOMING
YOUR
STRENGTHS

Also by
Lois P. Frankel, Ph.D.

Kindling the Spirit:

Acts of Kindness and Words
of Courage for Women

Women, Anger, and Depression:

Strategies for Self-Empowerment

OVERCOMING YOUR STRENGTHS

**8 Reasons Why
Successful People
Derail and How to
Get Back on Track**

Lois P. Frankel, Ph.D.

HARMONY BOOKS
New York

Author's Note

The names and identifying characteristics of actual coaching clients used throughout this book have been changed in order to maintain the confidentiality of the coaching relationship.

Grateful acknowledgment is made to the following for permission to reprint previously published material:

Consulting Psychologists Press, Inc.: for MBTI Preferences chart (pp. 72–73), modified and reproduced from *Introduction to Type in Organizations* by Sandra Krebs Hirsh and Jean M. Kummerow. Copyright © 1990 by Consulting Psychologists Press, Inc. All rights reserved. Further reproduction is prohibited without the publisher's written consent. Reprinted by permission of Consulting Psychologists Press, Inc., Palo Alto, CA 94303.

Communication Development Associates, Inc.: for Day to Day Communication Pie Chart (p. 84). Reprinted by permission of Communication Development Associates, Inc.

John Wiley & Sons, Inc.: "Preventing Individuals' Career Derailment" by Lois P. Frankel, Ph.D. from the Autumn 1994 issue of *Employment Relations Today,* volume 21, no. 3, pp. 295–305. Copyright © 1994 by John Wiley & Sons, Inc.

Published by Harmony Books, a division of Crown Publishers, Inc., 201 East 50th Street, New York, New York 10022.

Member of the Crown Publishing Group.

Random House, Inc. New York, Toronto, London, Sydney, Auckland

http://www.randomhouse.com/

HARMONY and colophon are trademarks of Crown Publishers, Inc.

Printed in the United States of America

Design by Deborah Kerner

Library of Congress Cataloging-in-Publication Data
Frankel, Lois P., 1953–
   Overcoming your strengths : 8 reasons why successful people derail and
   how to get back on track / by Lois P. Frankel. — 1st ed.
      1. Failure (Psychology)   2. Success—Psychological aspects.
   3. Attitude (Psychology)   I. Title.
   BF575.F14F73   1997
   158.1—dc21   96-48947

ISBN: 0-517-70414-5

10 9 8 7 6 5 4 3 2 1

First Edition

This book would not be possible without the coaching clients who allow me to enter their personal and professional lives and trust me enough to make the leap of faith required to overcome their strengths. It is to each one of you that this book is dedicated.

Acknowledgments

The most pleasant part of writing a book is when it comes time to acknowledge those people who helped and supported me through the process. My work is enhanced by the relationships I have with others and the input I receive from them. Therefore, I would like to thank the following people for so generously sharing with me their time, guidance, inspiration, and expertise.

Dr. Karen Otazo, who introduced me to the concept of coaching and provided me with the opportunity to work with the staff at ARCO as I developed my own coaching philosophy.

Susan Picascia, who had the integrity to forgo coauthoring this book so that she could be a mom to Alex and the generosity of spirit to continue to provide me with valuable insights and material used throughout this book.

Dr. Doug Andrews, assistant dean and chair of USC's Department of Business Communication, who graciously spent time brainstorming with me and acting as a sounding board for ideas.

Karen Flannery, manager of administration at Booz·Allen &

Hamilton, who conducted literature searches and fed me a continual stream of relevant information from her own reading and thirst for knowledge.

Ann Taylor and Beverly Anderson, who came to the rescue with their expertise in computer systems when I somehow managed to lose several chapters.

Carol DiPaolo, who for twenty-five years has been a dear friend, active advocate for my work, and editor extraordinaire.

The people at Harmony Books, especially Leslie Meredith and Sherri Rifkin, who had faith in my original concept and worked with me to produce an even better book than I originally envisioned.

Shirley Trissler, for the time spent researching biographical information and for encouraging and bearing with my neverending, often exhausting, pursuit of possibilities.

To each of you, and to the others in my network of extended family and friends, I extend a heartfelt thank-you. I hope that you know how very grateful I am for the gifts you have given me.

Contents

OVERCOMING YOUR STRENGTHS

Introduction

Have you ever wondered why certain people move ahead steadily through their careers while others stall or fall from their career tracks entirely? Some folks always seem to do and say the right thing, while others can't quite figure out what it takes to become and, more important, remain successful. Regardless of career path or position, most of us have experienced being on the sidelines and watching as less qualified colleagues get the choice assignments, promotions, or developmental opportunities that are intended to groom them for the next rung of the corporate ladder. We may grumble about the injustice of it all, but rarely do we take the time to examine *why* this happens and what we can do to make ourselves more competitive.

As a human resources consultant and corporate coach, working inside corporations and organizations worldwide, I've observed what makes certain people become and *remain* successful while others spin their wheels in what are at times lucrative but dead-end assignments. Corporations typically don't waste their time, energy, and resources on ne'er-do-wells, but they do put considerable effort into helping bright, capable, and competent people, who are stumbling over themselves, to succeed. The cost of turnover and finding these competent people is too high to do otherwise.

If you're reading this book, it is likely that your profile resembles the following: You are good at what you do, and may even be recognized for one or more particular strengths, but are somehow stalled or perhaps on the verge of *career derailment*. The term *derailment* was first used by researchers at the Center for Creative Leadership in Greensboro, North Carolina, to describe the process whereby fast-trackers are displaced from their successful career paths. The researchers estimate that 30 percent to 50 percent of high-potential managers and executives derail. Throughout this book the term *derailment* is used in a broad context to refer to people at *any* level in their careers who are faced with the possibility of unexpected career failure. Derailment occurs among secretaries with the same regularity as it does among executives—and for the same reasons.

Derailment is a change in career momentum. Otherwise successful people begin to stall in their careers, or fail entirely, for seemingly inexplicable reasons. People who work hard and have been rewarded for their contributions to a firm through promotions, job assignments, or special perks and incentives suddenly find themselves being overlooked for further recognition for no apparent reason. Their opinions may no longer be solicited, they may not be included in meetings with key people, or they may be given more routine, low-profile assignments than in the past. People suddenly feel invisible.

In exploring why some people derail while others remain on their career paths I found that people who experienced career derailment difficulties behaved in ways consistent with childhood expectations of them and relied almost exclusively on these behaviors for continued success. Typically, these are employees who have no history of job-related performance problems. In fact, they have frequently been identified as high-potential candidates and targeted for upward mobility.

Looking inside organizations that have downsized over the past decade, it is clear that the "survivors" of ongoing layoffs are frequently not the most technically proficient, best educated, or most productive. As corporations cut more closely to the bone, there appear to be few notable differences between those who are given their pink slips and those who remain. Examining the situation more closely, what emerges is a pattern of keeping people on staff who have the widest array of technical *and* interpersonal capabilities, rather than those who have very specific, but more limited, ones. This is what has become known as the "best-player" approach to downsizing: keeping those people who can function in a wide variety of areas and with a diverse group of people.

Managers are forced every day to make choices between keeping and laying off people who on the surface appear to be equally qualified. How, then, do they choose one over another? The answer lies in infrequently commented on, less tangible aspects of workplace behavior. Remarks like "Steve's a great worker, cranks out the work like no one else, but he doesn't get the big picture" or "Ann is one of our most talented engineers, but she doesn't get along with people" give us our greatest clues as to what contributes to one person's longevity and another's derailment. Derailment doesn't necessarily equate to automatic layoff or termination. People who are derailed frequently simply get overlooked again and again. Their input may be ignored or they or their departments may be overlooked for further growth opportunities. Whether they are laid off, ignored, or overlooked, the result is the same: career stagnation.

The common thread for people who derail is that they exhibit superior skill in a particular area *to the exclusion of developing comple-*

mentary ones. Even when a change in job assignment requires them to apply a different skill set, or when they see people around them develop in diverse areas, they *fail to notice* that they are limiting themselves and turn up the volume on those behaviors that they already do well, hoping that doing more of the same will save them! How do intelligent people neglect to notice something as important as their own lack of a diversified approach to other people and problem solving? The answer lies in the degree to which a strength was learned and reinforced in response to early childhood experiences.

Take for example Jamie, who comes from a home where Mom was an alcoholic and Dad, partially in response to Mom, was a workaholic. Jamie grew up knowing that her survival depended on taking good care of herself because there was no one else to do it for her. She learned to be independent and self-sufficient. Initially, she was a terrific employee. She was self-motivated and required little coaxing or direction. Eventually, however, Jamie began missing deadlines because she became overextended and failed to ask for assistance. Paradoxically, Jamie's strengths were what ultimately caused her to fail. She must learn to overcome her strengths, through the development of complementary skills, if she is to remain successful over the long term.

The truth is, we all have a little of Jamie in us. Maybe we didn't grow up in the same type of household, but we did grow up in environments that placed certain expectations and restrictions on our development. Whether we learned by word or deed that "children are to be seen and not heard," "you must do things yourself because no one else is to be trusted," or "never disagree with authority," those internalized messages affect our present behavior in the workplace. Our subconscious tells us that if our childhood survival depended on being quiet, independent, or compliant, then our adult well-being is certainly contingent on exhibiting those same behaviors.

Employees like Jamie need to be coached on how to add complementary skills to their existing strengths to help them stay on track. Enlightened companies realize that the cost of letting talented people go is way too high. Not only is there the cost of advertising, contracting firms, or interviewing, but there is also a cost to morale, productivity, and teamwork when someone is fired. Before making the decision to terminate employees like Jamie, these companies hire coaches to give the employees every opportunity to succeed. These companies realize that their own management may not always be the best coaches for their employees.

My coaching philosophy is simple: People should not *stop* engaging in behaviors that work for them, but rather identify the gaps in their repertoire of skills and fill them in with complementary strengths. People should remain essentially the same while adding new skills. It's a bit like learning a sport. When the golf coach suggests that the student change her grip he isn't asking her to fundamentally change who she is. He's only giving her a hint for how to be more successful on the golf course. If the student incorporates this hint into her game, she's rewarded with better scores.

The process of learning how to avoid derailment need not involve a lot of time or money. It isn't always necessary to hire an outside coach or spend countless years in psychotherapy. You can coach yourself to success by recognizing the eight most commonly made career mistakes described in the following chapters and learning the skills needed to overcome them. *Overcoming Your Strengths: 8 Reasons Why Successful People Derail and How to Get Back on Track* is designed for anyone who ever wondered why his or her career came to a screeching halt—and everyone who wants to prevent that from happening in the future. The Derailment Inventory in the following chapter will help you to assess your current derailment status, and suggestions throughout the book offer ways of staying or getting back on track. The key to using this book effectively lies in your willingness to critically assess your background, your behavior, and the direction of your career.

Throughout this book you'll find descriptions of how real-life employees nearly derailed as well as examples of high-profile personalities and historical figures who experienced premature career failures. Specific suggestions for overcoming your strengths are contained at the end of the subsequent chapters. You may discover that you have more in common with Chicago Bulls coach Phil Jackson or First Lady Hillary Rodham Clinton than you realized . . . and that even people who achieve great things need to continue to find ways to overcome their strengths.

Why Successful People Fail

Sarah was a senior accountant with an outstanding record of achievement in her midsize manufacturing firm until eight months ago, when she was promoted to manager of her department. Although she was able to produce high-quality results for the six years she was an individual contributor, she is currently foundering in her role as leader. She tries to do it all herself. Not only does she exclude others from the decision-making process, but she fails also to delegate. It appears that the skills that enabled her to accomplish so much at lower levels in the organization are the same ones that are now impeding her progress.

With only minor variations to the script, this scenario is played out daily in companies of all sizes around the globe. As a corporate coach, I'm called on to help employees like Sarah overcome obstacles to ongoing career success. My work typically begins with a phone call from a senior-level manager who wants coaching for someone who directly reports to him or her. The descriptions are similar: "I've got this employee who was *outstanding* when he first came on board. He was a real workhorse. We promoted him to manager, and now he's on probation. He needs help." When asked for a more detailed description of what the employee is doing wrong, the manager continues, "He's like a bull in a china shop, runs roughshod over people and embarrasses them in front of their peers. He just can't seem to understand that what it takes is a collaborative effort, not muscle."

Frequently, people like Sarah and the one this manager described fail without ever understanding why. Unfortunately, they often go on to other jobs and make the same mistakes again. They don't understand that those skills, characteristics, and qualities that contribute to success early in their careers are the same ones that ultimately serve to derail them once they reach higher levels of an organization or later stages of their careers. Paradoxically, the behaviors contributing to early career success are learned early in childhood as *defense mechanisms;* that is, they enabled people to survive what might have been difficult, traumatic, or demanding childhoods. In corporations, workers at every level of the business operation succeed by using the same survival skills they learned in childhood. These skills normally work, but only up to a point.

Repeating Past Behaviors

Whether the description is of someone who runs roughshod, does all the work instead of delegating, sees only the pieces of the puzzle instead of the bigger picture, has difficulty with authority, or is so easygoing that people walk all over him or her, it's a variation on the same theme: people who have not developed new skills that will provide balance to those skills that have contributed to early career success. If you are someone who continues to rely on behaviors that enabled you to survive childhood, despite the fact that *those behaviors have become counterproductive,* then you face the possibility of derailment.

Although many of Freud's theories have been questioned in recent years (and for good reason), he was right about the *repetition compulsion:* the tendency of human beings to return to past states, to repeat certain acts over and over again. And we repeat those acts over and over, even when they no longer work, until we understand what purpose they serve. We can all cite examples of people we know who marry several times, each time selecting the same type of partner and each time wondering why it doesn't work. For those of us on the outside looking in, it's abundantly clear why it doesn't work, but for the person making the choices it's Freud's repetition compulsion in action.

The choice of a partner often approximates the early childhood experience. That is, if Dad was an alcoholic, a woman may choose a husband who is either an alcoholic or in some similar way incapacitated. If Mom was depressed, her son may choose a depressed wife. This is not to say that these choices are conscious, because they most frequently are not. We make choices because they're *familiar,* and this familiarity enables us to know how to act in a given situation. Choosing a partner who is in some way familiar enables us to repeat the childhood behaviors we learned to survive—even though those behaviors are no longer functional!

Thus far the focus has been on developing survival skills in response to dysfunctional family behavior, but don't get the impression that people from these families are the only ones who develop such skills. Although current research suggests that nine out of ten people come from families of origin in which there is some type of dysfunction, these are not the only families for which survival skills are needed. You may come from that one functional family where everyone is a high achiever with advanced degrees in rocket science. Survival skills in this family may *look* different but still have the effect of obscuring necessary, complementary behaviors.

Defense mechanisms and survival skills aren't bad things. We all learned early on which behaviors pleased or satisfied our childhood primary caretakers, whether they were parents, nannies, grandparents, favorite teachers, or child-care workers. Even a pre-verbal child subconsciously knows that his or her survival depends on the caretaker. Therefore, repeating pleasing behavior was criti-cal to survival. It is logical, then, that we would assume that those behaviors that pleased the caretaker also would please others later in our lives. Most of us want to be loved and accepted, and often our behavior is motivated by this rather than an objective assess-ment of what the situation requires. Because the caretaker is also the first authority figure in our lives, we think that behaviors that pleased him or her will also please another authority figure—in the workplace that authority figure is the "boss."

What does all of this psychological jargon mean in today's cor-porate arena? Let's go back to Sarah for a moment. She is an out-standing individual contributor, but she can't quite empower others. Sarah's direct reports complain about her *grandstanding* (keeping the high-profile projects for herself), about *not trusting* them with an entire project, and about *micromanaging* their work. To understand these behaviors, we need to look at how they developed and what functional purpose they served in the past. As it turns out, Sarah was the oldest of six children. Both parents worked, and she had responsibility for taking care of her younger siblings after school, getting dinner started, baby-sitting during summer vaca-tions, and so on. She learned early in life that her survival—approval from her parents—was dependent on taking responsibility for what-ever needed to be done, without being asked. In order to juggle school and her chores at home, Sarah had to be organized, plan her activities in advance, and keep a close eye on her siblings.

In college Sarah was the ideal student. She not only had her papers done on time, she had them done in advance. She remained current with her studies while holding a part-time job from the second semester of her freshman year. As a young accountant, Sarah was every boss's dream. She showed initiative by anticipating what needed to be done and doing it thoroughly, paying close attention to detail, and with little supervision. Her performance reviews were, as might be expected, outstanding. The reward for her accomplishments as a superb worker was a promotion to a management position. As in most corporations, good individual performance in Sarah's company led to being promoted to leader of a team of employees. The problem inherent in this common practice is that the skills needed to lead a team are substantially different from those needed to succeed independently.

The repetition compulsion suggests that Sarah would naturally rely on the same skills that made her successful up to this point to ensure her success in her new assignment, and she did. What was perceived as grandstanding, not trusting others, and micromanaging was merely the repetition of the same childhood behaviors that contributed to her survival. She wasn't consciously keeping the high-profile projects to herself, nor was she intentionally trying to impede the growth of her staff by giving them only small pieces of projects. Given an assignment from upper management, she would simply plan out what had to be done and diligently go about doing it. She was more than happy to assist her direct reports with their routine tasks, in much the same way as she would help her younger siblings with their homework, but they perceived it as micromanaging. Sarah had no inkling that her behavior was unusual or inappropriate. It's almost as though she thought, "If it got me to this point, I should do more of it." And herein lies the problem for so many employees at all levels: not only doing what has worked in the past, but doing *more* of it.

Turning up the Volume

When faced with the prospect of failure, the child part of the adult psyche kicks into gear and *turns up the volume* on the same old behaviors, then wonders why there is static on the new station. The old station didn't have static! If controlling, planning, and doing the work herself worked for Sarah in the past, then certainly doing *more* of the same will work. As Sarah met with resistance from her staff, in the form of missing deadlines, withholding critical information, or doing work that wasn't up to acceptable standards, her survival instincts told her that she needed to engage *more* in the behaviors that contributed to her past success.

The obvious problem is that these were the same behaviors that now contributed to poor morale, low productivity, and lack of cooperation within her department. Doing more of the same only served to escalate the problem. It never occurred to Sarah that she exacerbated the problem by controlling and directing even more. In fact, because she had no alternative skills in her repertoire, she thought that she wasn't doing these things enough!

Promotions are not the only situations that can contribute to derailment; the inability to recognize and make the shift to the requirements of the organizational culture and movement from one company to another, one department to another, or one boss to another are others. Clearly, behaviors that are appropriate in one situation can become potential career derailers when applied in a different situation. If the culture of Sarah's company was more hierarchical, one in which people expected close supervision and little responsibility for entire projects, then her behavior would not have been considered problematic. In fact, she would continue to succeed using the behaviors she learned early in life.

Margaret Thatcher provides a familiar example of someone who derailed due to her failure to balance strengths with complementary skills when the situation called for it. As prime minister of England, Margaret Thatcher had a clear vision of where she wanted to take her country and how that should be accomplished. She was willing to take on tough and, at times, controversial issues. Her strengths earned her the nickname "The Iron Lady." Early in her tenure as prime minister she was welcomed by many citizens as one who stood by her convictions and who could lead the nation out of a difficult period of social and economic decline. She never faltered during the Falklands War and is characterized by her statement during the poll tax controversy, "You turn if you want to. The lady's not for turning."

So, what went wrong? Thatcher relied almost exclusively on behaviors learned early in childhood. Her independent, self-sufficient behaviors required complementary skills in consensus building and succeeding through cooperative efforts—skills that she not only never developed, but ones that she eschewed. Shortly after her election she proclaimed, "I am not a consensus politician. I am a conviction politician." And when the going got tough, Thatcher got tougher. She *turned up the volume* on her convictions. Throughout her tenure, she relied on the same skills she learned and relied on in childhood, and they ultimately failed her.

By all accounts Thatcher grew up in a joyless household. Outsiders report that there was never much gaiety or laughter in the home. Her mother was competent, but remote. Thatcher never really forged a relationship with her and rarely makes mention of her. It was her strict, work-oriented, and devoutly religious father with whom Thatcher aligned and to whom she credits her success. When she went to school and realized that other children actually had fun in their families, she asked him why their family never went on picnics, rode bicycles, or played games. His reply was, "Margaret, never do things or want to do things just because other people do them. Make up your own mind about what you are going to do and persuade people to go your way." Clearly, she learned that lesson well. So well that she was alienated from her peers throughout her school years and to this day claims no close friends with the exception of her husband.

In the corporate arena, an example of an employee turning up the volume is one who moves from a department that places high value on teamwork, collaboration, and consensus to another department in the same organization that requires independent decision making, quick turnaround, and minimal interaction among team members. Because the employee came from a family where harmony was the norm, it is expected that he or she would be successful in the first department; its requirements match his or her behavioral schemata. Moving to the latter department, the person will be unsure of what behaviors are expected and will, most likely, rely on the people skills that secured career success thus far. When at first they don't work, he or she will likely engage in the behaviors to an even greater degree. The employee will flounder if he or she doesn't recognize the need to engage in alternative, situationally expected behavior. As the individual tries to reach consensus and build collaborative relationships, he or she may meet with resistance from his or her new coworkers. The likely method for dealing with this resistance is to turn up the volume even further on the affiliative skills—and wonder why there is static on the line.

High Tolerance Levels

Another aspect of relying on early childhood behaviors involves the ability to tolerate bad employment situations or poor leadership. When confronted with a boss who is unreasonable (or downright impossible), employees will tolerate those behaviors that are congruent with their primary family experience. At the end of a leadership workshop, Tim took the facilitator aside and asked how to cope with a boss who made unreasonable demands, embarrassed him in front of others, and never gave any praise. When asked "Does he remind you of anyone?" Tim hesitated for a moment while thinking and finally replied, "My father."

You may find that you have a high level of tolerance for inappropriate behaviors that are familiar to you, especially if feelings about being treated in a particular way haven't been worked through in psychotherapy or other developmental opportunities, such as attending workshops, taking classes, or reading self-help books. You may seek approval from authority, can't see when you're being treated unfairly or inappropriately and, therefore, assume responsibility for making the situation better. This is another instance in which behaviors that worked in the past to assure survival will be turned up in volume.

Rita worked for a boss who confided in her about myriad personal problems with her children, parents, and her spouse. On some occasions, the boss would go into Rita's office, close the door, and break down and sob. Rita said she was uncomfortable being used as a confidante in this manner because it prohibited her from going to the boss with her own work-related problems. She felt sorry for her boss and didn't want to burden her any more than necessary. As a result, Rita was left having to figure out for herself how to resolve problems and create programs for which she had little experience. Because she grew up with a mother who needed excessive attention and was histrionic, Rita felt as responsible for her boss as she did for her mother. She turned up the volume on her listening and caretaking behaviors in order to soothe the boss. The child in the workplace needed to make things better, never expecting that she was entitled to leadership and direction from her boss.

Tim and Rita tolerated bad employment situations because the situations were familiar and they knew how to survive them. However, their performance and self-esteem suffered from lack of mentoring and growth opportunities expected from people in management positions. Both employees eventually left their positions and their companies once they understood the dynamics and decided not to be controlled by old behaviors that have outlived their usefulness.

The Corporate Playing Field

It is sometimes helpful to draw an analogy between a sports playing field and the corporate arena. Just as in sports, there is a playing field in companies and organizations. The field has bounds that mark the area in which players must operate. When you go out of bounds in sports you are called out, foul, lose a point, or lose control of the ball. There is typically some type of penalty for going off the playing field. The same holds true in companies. You must understand the boundaries of the playing field in order to win the game.

A major difference that presents a unique problem is that the bounds of corporate playing fields change from company to company, department to department within the same company, and even from boss to boss within a company. It's easy to go out of bounds when they change so frequently. Successful corporate players scope out the playing field and adjust their behavior accordingly. In other words, they remain in bounds for *each given situation.*

Although the corporate playing field clearly denotes the area in which it expects employees to operate, there are a number of inherent dangers. The field may be artificially narrowed based on factors relating to gender, ethnicity, age, or other subjective factors. When the field narrows, it becomes easier to go out of bounds. For example, the playing field for men in the area of emotionality is narrower than it is for women. The range of emotions that they are permitted to express is narrower than that permitted for women. Similarly, the playing field for women in the area of assertiveness is narrower than for their male counterparts. Displaying the same assertive behavior as men may get them called out of bounds. All corporate players need to be aware of their own biases that may artificially narrow the playing field for their colleagues and make every effort to create a more even field for everyone.

There is also the danger that people will play the game too carefully, never taking the kinds of risks that might put them out of bounds. In an environment such as this, creativity is stifled. As in sports, you must take calculated risks and play the game toward the edge of the bounds, but intentionally decide when the risk of going out of bounds is worth what will potentially be gained by it.

Once again, it is about balance. If you are someone who constantly goes out of bounds, don't be surprised if you are eventually called out. On the other hand, if you always play the corporate game safely within bounds, you may not be adding the value required for long-term success. People who avoid premature career derailment are those who (1) know where the bounds are and recognize that they narrow and widen with different circumstances, (2) play the corporate game taking calculated risks, and (3) balance the risks with the eight behaviors described in this book.

The Eight Most Common Reasons Why Successful People Fail

Consider the following workplace conversation:

Al: *Did you hear about Kathy's promotion?*

Barbara: *Did I ever. I've been here three years longer than Kathy and work twice as hard. I should have been the one given that promotion.*

Al: *I thought for sure this one had your name on it. Kathy's only been in her position for eighteen months. Seems like she hardly warmed up the chair. She must know people over at corporate.*

Barbara: *Not only does she know them, she spends more time meeting with them than doing her work. She's always going to this committee meeting and that presentation. If she spent half as much time in her office working as she does schmoozing, she could get something done.*

Al: *Yeah. It's people like us who keep this place going and people like her who get all the credit. Do you know that she even has time to take her staff members out to lunch for their birthdays?*

Barbara: *That's what I mean. She's so busy getting everyone else to do her work that of course she has time for all that stuff. The HR vice pres-*

ident asked me to be on the personnel review committee, and I turned
him down flat. If I don't keep close tabs on my staff nothing gets done.

Al: *I know what you mean. I've got my schedule just about where I want*
it now, and I'm not willing to change it for anyone. Those committees
take up too much time.

Sound familiar? While Barbara and Al are busy micromanaging, doing the work themselves, and sticking close to their offices, behaviors that have worked for them up until now in their careers, people like Kathy are expanding their repertoires of business behavior. You may have heard people talk about the differences between "careerists" and "achievers." The former manage their careers, and the latter get the work done. In fact, both are important elements of remaining on your career track. You can't simply focus on your career to the exclusion of accomplishing your work, and you can't only accomplish your work without paying attention to your career development. It is a combination of specific behaviors that ultimately leads to career success.

It should go without saying, but I'll say it anyway to make it clear: *There is no substitute for technical competence.* It is the foundation on which all the other behaviors referred to in this book rely. Without technical competence you build a career on quicksand. The problem is that most people who derail rely on technical competence to the exclusion of all other necessary behaviors. They think that expertise in their field should be enough to maintain their careers. This may have been true in 1960 or 1970, but it is far from true in today's competitive workplace.

People who possess the technical competence but prematurely derail from their career paths do so because of the following factors. They

1. Overlook the importance of people.
2. Do not function effectively as part of a team.

3. Fail to focus on image and communication.
4. Are insensitive to the effect they have on others.
5. Have difficulty working with authority.
6. Have too broad or too narrow vision.
7. Are indifferent to customer or client needs.
8. Work in isolation.

Most derailed people fail to build skills in more than just one area. For example, the inability to function effectively as part of a team may be related to working in isolation. Or, having difficulty working with authority may cause you to be indifferent to client or customer needs. The Derailment Inventory at the end of this chapter will help you to determine which specific areas you may need to work on in order to prevent or overcome derailment. I urge you to take the inventory and to use it in determining which chapters might have the most meaning for you personally. Also, examine your workplace behaviors in light of early childhood experiences and determine which complementary skills the inventory suggests are required to be a fully functioning adult. If you look only at your scores, you miss out on the opportunity to understand your behavior in a fuller context. Here's where many career coaches fail. They focus on changing behavior, not understanding the purpose the behavior serves and *how it has contributed to success in the past.*

The chart following the Derailment Inventory ties together the eight most common reasons why successful people fail with possible early childhood experiences contributing to learned behaviors. Because people develop strength in a particular area for any number of reasons, it is impossible to list every combination of experiences contributing to every strength. Use the chart as a point of reference to begin thinking about how and why you developed in certain areas and not others. You may even want to add your own unique experiences to those listed.

Factors to Consider in Assessing and Changing Behavior

Critically examining your behavior is no easy task, but it can have immense payoffs, both at work and home, over the long term. There are several key points to keep in mind before you respond to the Derailment Inventory.

• *People don't intentionally behave inappropriately or ineffectively.* To hear managers tell it, you would think that the behaviors of their employees are intentional attempts to undermine their efforts. As a result, they wind up labeling and blaming employees, and employees internalize these labels as undeniable truths—truths that impede learning alternative behaviors. I don't think that there is a person on earth who gets up in the morning, pours a cup of coffee, and says, "I think I'll go to work today and make a huge, costly mistake." My belief is that the large majority of people act with the best of intentions. If you knew how to do things differently, you would. The problem is, you can't know what you don't know!

It is crucial to separate the act from the actor. Someone who hasn't learned how to build affiliative relationships isn't a bad person simply because he or she hasn't learned this skill. Generally, the reason that a particular skill hasn't been learned is that, historically, it wasn't important in the scheme of things. As you use the Derailment Inventory to assess your current skills and those that you'd like to add to your repertoire, avoid the tendency to become your own "critical parent." Keep in mind that we all have strengths and developmental areas. There are no right or wrong answers. Praise yourself for being open to change, and allow plenty of room for initially falling short of the mark.

• *People do best the things for which they have been rewarded in the past.* What does the Derailment Inventory indicate are your greatest strengths? Think about these strengths as overdeveloped survival skills, and ask yourself these three questions:

- Who wanted (or needed) me to act in this way?
- How was I rewarded when I did?
- What happened if I didn't?

Use the chart that follows the Derailment Inventory to help stimulate your thinking in this area. This exercise will help you to demystify the part that your strengths played while you were growing up and enable you to examine why other behaviors weren't as important.

- *Be willing to take calculated risks.* Examine your scores and look for the items for which you rated yourself "3" or "4." These are behaviors that may not come naturally to you or ones that you may even have been discouraged from exhibiting in childhood. Developing complementary skills may mean being uncomfortable in the beginning. As people progress through the stages of initial learning they feel inadequate, impatient, or insecure and revert back to more familiar behaviors as a means of coping. It is only through the willingness to engage in unfamiliar, uncomfortable behavior, and to stick with it, that complementary skills can be developed.

- *Don't do anything less. Expand your skill set.* Successful people don't fail because they're not good at what they do. They fail when they can't see the complementary behaviors that must be developed in response to a new challenge or situation. If you, for example, focus on being less critical or less task oriented, you'll naturally be uncomfortable with doing less of what you know best. Instead, think about the skills that you need to add to your repertoire of workplace behaviors to be more effective. It's all about having a balanced skill set.

Sarah's manager didn't want her to completely cease getting

the work cranked out. He wanted her to achieve more balance in her leadership style. Employees frequently leave feedback sessions feeling more confused than when they first went in. They become fearful of engaging in what's described as the "problem behavior" *at all* and wind up going to the opposite extreme. Continue engaging in those behaviors where you rated yourself a "1" or "2" as you develop comfort and familiarity in those areas where you rated yourself lower.

• *Successful people are good observers of people and events.* In most cases, people change positions, companies, departments, bosses, or jobs, and no one bothers to tell them what is expected of them. It's as though they hear a tape playing over and over, telling them how to behave, and they try harder and harder to act consistently. The only problem is that the tape is usually an old one, developed in response to childhood needs, not present realities. The people who succeed at career transitions are the ones who observe how others in the new situation are acting and adjust their behavior accordingly. When in Rome, do as the Romans do.

This is not to say that people should be chameleons, giving up the essence of who they are from situation to situation. They should, however, take note of cultural customs such as how people dress, whether they have lunch with coworkers, and the kind of social interactions that go on in the office. A little bit of accommodation can go a long way toward the perception of "fitting in."

• *Assure success through a development plan and ongoing feedback.* Just as you wouldn't build a house without a plan, neither should you count on personal or professional development without one. The common theme to motivational speeches is the fact that the person had a vision of what he or she wanted and a plan for attaining it. Success isn't accidental. Based on the Derailment Inventory, decide the two or three skills that are most important to add to your repertoire and determine how you will achieve them. Be sure to identify the resources you will require in the process: people, classes, books, and experiences.

One tip you might consider is to let others know the changes you're attempting to make. This way, people will actually look for and notice the behavior change, and increase the likelihood of giving you positive feedback. Once you have your development plan, ask someone you trust to review it with you and to give you feedback as to how you're doing. Let him or her know what you're trying to accomplish and how you would like to receive your feedback. Then, on a regular basis, sit down and review progress. Discuss where you encountered difficulty, brainstorm methods for overcoming obstacles, revise the plan, and, perhaps most important, reward wins—even small ones—with a mental pat on the back, thumbs-up, or more tangible self-indulgences. Remember, you're most likely to repeat behaviors for which you've been rewarded.

The goal is not to make you an armchair psychologist, but rather to help you to look at your strengths in the context of your experiences and motives. We are not one-dimensional objects. We bring to the workplace a host of multifaceted intentions, which, when developed in light of organizational needs, can contribute significantly to work's synergistic process and the satisfaction we gain from it. When we view ineffective behaviors as overdeveloped, purposeful strengths, they no longer seem like insurmountable obstacles—and we no longer feel like failures.

Each of the following chapters fully explores the behaviors that lead to career derailment and provides a strategy for avoiding those pitfalls. Well-known historical and contemporary figures who derailed at some point in their careers are used as a means of illustrating why certain behaviors are developed early in childhood as survival skills and the effect of such behaviors on careers. Also provided are examples of behaviors based on encounters with real-life employees and suggestions for how to build complementary skills in each of these areas. At the end of each chapter is a list of ways that you can develop skill in the area on which the chapter focuses. Even if many of them may be a stretch for you, I urge you to consider each one as a simple and economical way to begin expanding your repertoire of workplace behaviors. You may come up with other suggestions for yourself based on what you have just read. The Resources, at the end of the book, contain references for many of the books, workshops, and inventories mentioned throughout. Combined, these serve to illuminate how successful people stay that way and how you can overcome your strengths.

DERAILMENT INVENTORY

To determine where you currently stand in the derailment process, use the scale below to answer each of the following questions as candidly as possible. Even if it is difficult to answer a particular item, do not leave it unanswered.

1 = Highly descriptive of me or my situation.
2 = Descriptive of me or my situation.
3 = Somewhat descriptive of me or my situation.
4 = Not descriptive of me or my situation.

1. ____ Others describe me as a real "people person."
2. ____ I prefer to work as part of a team rather than work independently of others.
3. ____ When I speak, people pay close attention to my ideas and opinions and I see them later used or implemented.
4. ____ I see myself as even-tempered.

5. ____ When I have a logical reason for it, I don't have a problem with expressing a viewpoint different from my management's.

6. ____ When working on a project, I enjoy taking time out now and then to reassess its direction and my own method of approaching it.

7. ____ I find it a challenge to overcome initial obstacles to achievement.

8. ____ I spend at least some portion of each week networking with colleagues.

9. ____ I spend some part of each workday engaged in small talk with coworkers.

10. ____ I enjoy working collaboratively as a member of a team.

11. ____ I believe how you say something is equally as important as what you say.

12. ____ I know the difference between passive, aggressive, and assertive behavior, and I would describe my workplace behavior as assertive.

13. ____ If I see managers making decisions that I believe might be harmful to our firm, I offer my opinion about these decisions.

14. ____ It doesn't bother me when my boss interrupts a project I'm working on to add new and sometimes different elements to it.

15. ____ I find it personally rewarding to be of service to others.

16. ____ I belong to professional organizations and attend their meetings with enough regularity to know the other members.

17. ____ I know most of my coworkers on more than just a professional basis.

18. ____ I believe that my individual contribution to a project is enhanced by securing input from others.

19. ____ I think before speaking to make certain my comments are presented in the best light possible.

20. ____ Others would describe me as someone who has definite opinions but who also solicits and listens to the opinions of others.

21. ____ People would describe me as someone who can independently assess management decisions and offer alternative perspectives when appropriate.

22. ____ Others describe me as someone with a vision of the future.

23. ____ It is unusual for me to say "no can do" to a request.

24. ____ A few times each month, I'm invited to join key players on my team or in my organization for lunch.

25. ____ I am often successful where others fail because of the relationships I have with others.

26. ____ I enjoy projects that call on people with different perspectives to work together.

27. ____ I shop for my own work clothes and keep in mind what would "fit in" so that I can gear my purchases in that direction.

28. ____ Diplomacy is one of my greatest strengths.

29. ____ When management solicits my opinion, they know I'll respond candidly.

30. ____ I balance task accomplishment with finding new and creative ways of doing things.

31. ____ I consciously think about how I can add value to my organization.

32. ____ I'd say I'm pretty well tuned into my firm's grapevine.

33. ____ I don't have an inordinate need for everyone to like me.

34. ____ I'm energized by the exchange of ideas that come from brainstorming with others.

35. ____ People have told me that I'm a good public speaker.

36. ____ I rarely shoot the messenger when I don't like the message.

37. ____ I believe it's more important to be honest with my manager than to placate him or her for the sake of staying in his or her good graces.

38. ____ It is important to me that things be done correctly as well as on time.

39. ____ The fact that I enjoy my work is typically evident in the upbeat attitude that I display when doing it.

40. ____ I have colleagues in positions similar to mine in other divisions within my own firm, or at other firms, with whom I regularly interact to exchange ideas and keep abreast of issues pertinent to my job.

DERAILMENT INVENTORY SCORE SHEET

To score your inventory, first transfer your numerical responses from the questionnaire itself to the columns below. Please notice that the item numbers within each column are not in order, so be sure to put your response next to the correct item number. After you have transferred your answers, making sure you have answered each question, tally each column separately, then add each of the column subtotals together for an overall inventory total.

I PEOPLE SKILLS	II. TEAM-WORK	III. IMAGE/COMMU-NICATION	IV. PERSON-ALITY	V. WORKING WITH AUTHORITY	VI. DETAIL VS. BIG PICTURE	VII. CAN-DO ATTITUDE	VIII. NET-WORKING
1. ____	2. ____	3. ____	4. ____	5. ____	6. ____	7. ____	8. ____
9. ____	10. ____	11. ____	12. ____	13. ____	14. ____	15. ____	16. ____
17. ____	18. ____	19. ____	20. ____	21. ____	22. ____	23. ____	24. ____
25. ____	26. ____	27. ____	28. ____	29. ____	30. ____	31. ____	32. ____
33. ____	34. ____	35. ____	36. ____	37. ____	38. ____	39. ____	40. ____

SUBTOTALS: ____ ____ ____ ____ ____ ____ ____ ____

INVENTORY TOTAL: ____

INTERPRETING YOUR SCORES

The subtotal of each column tells you areas in which you need to expand your complementary skills and areas where your current strengths lie. The total score tells you how close to derailment you are. It is entirely possible to need development in one or two specific areas without being career derailed.

If each column subtotals:	or	Your total score is:	
5–8		40–75	You're right on track! Examine those areas where you rated yourself 1 or 2 and consciously try to continue engaging in those specific behaviors.
9–13		76–115	Fine-tuning may be needed to stay on track. Review those questions where you gave yourself 3 or 4 and add those complementary skills to your existing repertoire.
14–17		116–145	*Warning!* You're dangerously close to derailing. Time to do a serious self-assessment and expand your skill set.
18–20		146–160	Whether you know it or not, you're seriously derailed. Seek help (a career coach, a mentor) to get your career back on track.

Childhood Experiences Contributing
to Strengths and Developmental Areas

DERAILMENT FACTOR:	PERSON/BEHAVIOR COMMONLY DESCRIBED AS:	OVERDEVELOPED SKILL/BEHAVIOR:	POSSIBLE CHILDHOOD CAUSATIVE FACTORS:
1. POOR PEOPLE SKILLS	A loner Socially inept Uncomfortable in social situations Unfriendly Lacks insight Aloof Avoids people contact Inordinate need to be liked	Technical brilliance Ability to work independently Exactness, precision, and accuracy People pleasing Tolerance for bad situations	Value placed on accomplishments Rewarded for grades, achievements Overly protective parenting Intelligent, ostracized by classmates Economic status lower than peers' Physical impairment Narcissistic parenting Conditional love and acceptance
2. INABILITY TO WORK AS PART OF A TEAM	Doesn't see interdependent linkages Grandstands Doesn't include others in decision making Hoards information Impatient	Individual contributions Ability to work unsupervised Completion orientation	Oldest in family or only child Alcoholism in family Both parents worked outside the home Rewarded for self-reliance High-achiever expectations
3. INATTENTION TO IMAGE AND COMMUNICATION STYLE	Doesn't think before speaking Wears cheap clothes	Independent thinking Straight shooting Risk taking	Wasn't listened to Given little parental guidance

DERAILMENT FACTOR:	PERSON/BEHAVIOR COMMONLY DESCRIBED AS:	OVERDEVELOPED SKILL/BEHAVIOR:	POSSIBLE CHILDHOOD CAUSATIVE FACTORS:
3. INATTENTION TO IMAGE AND COMMUNICATION STYLE (cont.)	Dresses as one would for a party Can't get to the point, rambles on Uncomfortable making presentations Lacks confidence Like a bull in a china shop Seems insincere Not credible	Humility	Neglected Limited world exposure
4. INSENSITIVE TO ONE'S EFFECT ON OTHERS	A bully Muscle level too high Turns people off Inconsiderate of others Too loud Knows it all Doesn't listen	Doing whatever it takes Perseverance Autonomous functioning Self-confidence	Critical parental messages Parents with emotional problems Lack of positive reinforcement Conditional love High-achiever expectations
5. DIFFICULTY WORKING WITH AUTHORITY	Argumentative with management Embarrasses management in front of others Afraid to speak up in front of superiors Doesn't point out potential problems	Independence Respect for hierarchy Support for traditional values	Overly critical or controlling parenting Narcissistic parenting Physical or emotional abuse

DERAILMENT FACTOR:	PERSON/BEHAVIOR COMMONLY DESCRIBED AS:	OVERDEVELOPED SKILL/BEHAVIOR:	POSSIBLE CHILDHOOD CAUSATIVE FACTORS:
6. TOO BROAD OR TOO NARROW VISION	Narrowly focused One-track mind Can't juggle multiple tasks simultaneously Unable to turn ideas into reality Unrealistic	Determination Task orientation Creativity	Ritualistic family behavior Alcoholism or physical abuse Unpredictable or chaotic environment Absence of boundaries or norms
7. LACK OF CONCERN FOR CUSTOMER OR CLIENT NEEDS	A "naysayer" Fails to add value Identifies problems, not solutions Not a self-starter Requires inordinate supervision Risk-averse	Critical thinking Attention to detail Careful, deliberate behavior Compliance	Controlled environment Predetermined career path "Powerless" parental attitude
8. WORKS IN ISOLATION	Isn't well connected Doesn't have the contacts in place Doesn't keep up professionally	Ability to work independently High task orientation Makes good use of time	Rewarded for self-reliance Not encouraged to join clubs or teams Overly attached to primary caretaker

Overlooking the Importance of People

BUILD STRONG ONE-ON-ONE RELATIONSHIPS

An early coaching experience involved a woman whom I'll call Diane. She was the assistant to the vice president of human resources at a large corporation. When the vice president called me about Diane, he told me that she was an outstanding assistant. He found no fault with the quality of her work. The problem was that Diane's peers didn't want to work with her. They found her stand-offish and difficult to work with. Despite the fact that she was technically competent, she would soon derail if she didn't stop creating morale problems in the department. Diane arrived at our first coaching session looking every bit the executive assistant. Trim, neatly groomed, and impeccably dressed, she appeared to be the very model of professionalism. As we became acquainted with one another through initial superficial conversation, it was noted that she spoke with a clarity and confidence that belied her age (she was in her late twenties). When she was asked what she thought the problem was for which she had been asked to receive coaching, she didn't have a clue. She said she just wanted to do the best job possible and tried to be perfect so as to make her boss look good. A light went on.

The "package" that Diane presented was indeed one of perfection. On the surface, you could find no fault with her image or communication, but my hunch was (and it later proved to be accurate) that she overrelied on her ability to be perfect for her boss to the exclusion of other critical workplace behaviors. I explored this with her by changing tack. She was asked what she did for fun outside of work. What was she like when she wasn't being perfect? Unexpectedly, this unleashed a flood of emotion. Diane tearfully said that she didn't have much of a life outside of work. She arrived at work early, so as to be prepared for the busy day that always ensued working for this executive, and she typically didn't leave until 7:00 P.M. By the time she made the hour commute home, she was exhausted; she would have something to eat and then fall into bed.

After carefully listening to her explain that she had not had a significant relationship in a number of years, nor was there one on the horizon, I asked Diane if perhaps her need for affiliation was fulfilled at work with friends and colleagues. Her answer was no. She worked through her lunch hours and didn't want to waste the company's time and money on idle chat or gossip with her coworkers. She did notice that the other women on the floor seemed to spend time engaged in casual conversation, which was fine for them, but she herself didn't have the time to spare, nor did she think it was right.

What others interpreted as standoffishness, or being difficult to deal with, was really just Diane's need to be the perfect employee. Having grown up in a strict Norwegian household, she developed the defense mechanism of striving for perfection early in life to ward off critical comments from her parents and older siblings. The need to be perfect underscored not only her work-place relationships, but her personal ones as well. One reason for not having close friends or intimate relationships was that no one ever measured up to her high standards. Even though she never said anything to her colleagues, they picked up on the fact that she was critically assessing them. She found their personal conversations self-indulgent and didn't feel that anyone else worked as hard as she did, which was in fact true. No one else shared her compulsive need for perfection.

When Technical Expertise Ceases to Be Enough

Diane provides a wonderful example of someone who, despite technical competence, was on the verge of premature derailment. An infrequently talked about fact of business life is that at some point in most people's careers, technical expertise ceases to be the key factor contributing to success. We *build* our reputations early in our careers on competence. We *remain* successful, however, based on a combination of competence and the eight factors described in this book. Once we have proved our technical abilities in our respective fields, competence becomes a given—something that others can depend and rely on, but, after a point, not something that necessarily moves us forward. It is as though our competence reaches the point of diminishing returns. The mistake that many people make is to focus exclusively on gaining increased technical skill to the exclusion of developing other complementary workplace behaviors.

Review the following checklist to see how well you build one-on-one relationships. Ideally one would check every item (here as with each checklist contained in subsequent chapters). The fewer items checked, the greater likelihood that this is a potential developmental area for you.

_____ I know the names of the people on my floor.

_____ I can usually tell when something is troubling a colleague.

_____ I'm comfortable making small talk with coworkers.

_____ I enjoy the opportunity to meet socially with coworkers.

_____ I tend to go out of my way for colleagues—even if I see no immediate benefit.

_____ I see building relationships as equally important to accomplishing my job tasks.

_____ Others would describe me as a good listener.

_____ I make it a point to spend some part of each day engaged in casual conversation with coworkers.

_____ I know the names of the husbands, wives, significant others, and children of my coworkers.

_____ I don't consider sharing personal information or topics of common interest as a waste of company time.

_____ I know the names of my colleagues' administrative assistants.

In today's competitive job market, employers are careful to choose people for their past experience, education, and previous on-the-job success. In other words, they select people who are good at what they do. Once on the job, however, when the playing field is level with equally qualified employees, it is the more subtle behaviors that differentiate the fast-trackers from those who remain stagnant. Those with superior interpersonal skills, combined with technical capability, are perceived as a more valuable asset than those who exhibit only technical competence. Through the ability to establish positive working relationships we secure the cooperation of the people we need to accomplish our tasks and further the organization's goals. These interpersonal skills also help us to develop the goodwill of clients and customers and a network of people on whom we can rely for the skills and information required to function effectively.

In Diane's case, coaching alone wasn't sufficient to help her prevent derailment. The presence of a deep-seated need for perfection suggests intrapersonal conflicts that require professional counseling. Fortunately, when this was recommended to Diane she was open to the idea and followed up on it. Her coaching sessions focused on several specific things that she could do immediately to change the impression others had of her. She is a good example of someone who had several overlapping areas of development. Diane needed not only to do a better job of building one-on-one relationships, but also to be a better team player and begin to think about the importance of networking. My work with her addressed all three areas.

Her first assignment was to spend no less than fifteen minutes each day engaged in casual conversation with a different coworker—even if she had to force herself to do it. She was asked to get to know her colleagues personally, to find out what outside interests and hobbies they had, the names of their children, and what made them tick. This is no easy task for people like Diane. It makes them feel as if they are somehow robbing the company coffers, when in reality they are investing in relationships that have a long-term benefit to the company. Building such relationships enables the work to be done more efficiently, with less sabotage and higher team morale.

Similarly, it was recommended that Diane take a lunch break at least once a week and use the time for something she enjoyed. The adage "all work and no play makes Jill a dull girl" was certainly true in Diane's case. Part of what made it so difficult for her to talk to others was that she felt she had nothing to say. She had become so immersed in her work that she was oblivious to outside interests. Diane decided to join a nearby gym and work out. At the gym, she met several people with whom she shared common interests, eventually became friends with them, and started to have lunch and socialize with them after work.

In an effort to coach her in how to be a better team player and networker, it was recommended that Diane offer help to coworkers rather than spend time perfecting and fail-safing her already good work. She could put her compulsive work behaviors to good use by extending herself to those who needed her assistance. In other words, she could win back their regard by making not only her boss look good, but her colleagues as well. In the process, she was building what is described as *network reciprocity*—the exchange of services and favors within formal and informal networks. The importance of networks is discussed in detail in Reason #8, Working in Isolation, but for now suffice it to say that Diane had to identify and participate in the quid pro quo of her workplace relationships. Diane worked hard to change the perceptions of others and successfully learned how to overcome her strengths. She has been promoted to a new position, has many friends both at work and home, and reports that the quality of her life is now better than she has ever known it to be.

Understanding the Quid Pro Quo

In nearly every relationship there is something called a *quid pro quo*—something given in exchange for something else. Without realizing it, we are exchanging things with people all the time. Inherent to every relationship there is a quid pro quo. Many relationships fail when the quid pro quo isn't recognized or when it changes without the consent or acknowledgment of one or both of the parties involved. I remember working with one woman who was concerned with her troubled employment history. It seemed that she had no trouble getting a job. In fact, she was never without one for long. She was technically competent, physically attractive, and interpersonally capable. Clearly, she presented well in interviews and secured most of the jobs for which she interviewed. The problem was that once she was in the job, she became quickly dissatisfied and disillusioned. Her employers wouldn't give her challenging assignments or recognize her technical capability.

In an effort to uncover what the cause of the problem really was, I asked her to role-play an interview with me. Was I surprised to find that this professional woman turned into a femme fatale in the role play! Her normally assertive demeanor was replaced by what I would intentionally describe as a *sweet* disposition. The slight Southern accent with which she normally spoke became more pronounced. She was coy, acquiescent, and charming.

It was apparent that the woman secured the job based on one set of behaviors but unwittingly changed them once she was inside the company. In other words, the quid pro quo changed. Her employer expected one thing based on the interview and, instead, got something else. She didn't present as, nor was she selected for being, an assertive, upwardly mobile career woman in the interview. Her employers selected her for the behavior she presented, not what she became once employed. This created a chasm between what *they* wanted and what *she* wanted. There was obviously nothing wrong with what she wanted, but it was not the message she gave during her interviews. When the quid pro quo changed, unbeknownst to the parties involved, it created turmoil and unfulfilled expectations for both.

Part of building successful relationships at work involves identifying the quid pro quo between you and everyone with whom you interact, and working to assure that everyone's—including your own—needs get met. Some might say that this business of quid pro quo sounds awfully manipulative. On the contrary! It's an honest businesslike assessment of what you have to offer others and what you need from them. We trade on relationships all day long without ever realizing or discussing it. Say a month ago you asked me to cover for you at a meeting so that you could attend to a problem with one of your children, and I willingly complied. A while later, I needed some research done that only you know how to do and you gladly obliged. Neither of us was counting the chips we had collected with each trade, but they had accumulated in our accounts. The trick is to always have more chips in your account than you need—and this can't be done manipulatively; it can only be done through a generosity of spirit. To do otherwise would soil the integrity of the relationship.

The value of the quid pro quo was apparent during a training program, when a small group that was working on an assignment decided that they needed a particular piece of audiovisual equipment that projects written material directly from a laptop onto a screen. One participant said that she thought she could arrange it and excused herself to make a call. I mentally noted that there was little chance of getting the equipment on time—their presentation was just a few hours away. Ninety minutes later the equipment arrived. When I took the woman aside to ask her how she managed to get it so quickly, she smiled and said, "I've done this man many favors. We have a good relationship."

Dr. Karen Otazo, formerly manager of training and development at ARCO, once reminded me of the value of having an account full of chips. We were working together on a project and I made a mistake with some aspect of it. I called to let her know about it and indicated that I was willing to do whatever was necessary to make it right. "Not to worry," she assured me. "Your bank account is full." I knew what she meant. I could *afford* to make a mistake, because the positive aspects of our relationship and all of the error-free work I had done superseded this error.

Besides overlooking mistakes, covering at meetings, or conducting research, what else gets traded in the workplace? You would be surprised. Here's a list that one workshop group came up with in less than five minutes:

Information	Quality Service	Promotions
Lunch	Friendship	Quick Turnaround
Gossip	Technical Know-how	A Listening Ear
Priority	Raises	Help
Muscle/Brawn	Influence	Information on Jobs in Other Firms
Feedback	Gifts	
Public Praise	Personal Concern	Heads Up (Advance Notice)
		Information on Upcoming Job Openings

It is important to remember that *once you need a relationship, it's too late to build it.* This is what makes building relationships on an ongoing basis so important. Again, it can't be done simply for the purpose of knowing that you might have to call on it at some time. It must be done because you value people and your relationships with them. Absent this, others will detect a lack of genuineness, and perhaps a bit of manipulation, and never fully engage in a relationship with you.

Every so often I hear someone claim that he or she just doesn't care about building relationships. It always strikes me as oddly incongruous. These same people who claim not to care frequently exhibit behaviors that indicate they care very much. It is their defense mechanisms speaking. After years of being hurt by others, or not having much success in building relationships, they build impenetrable walls that they dare others to break through. In other cases, people who claim not to care about others are the same ones who don't care much about themselves. They don't pay attention to their own needs and certainly don't expect others to fulfill them. Whatever the reason, it is critical to overcome real or perceived indifference to the people with whom you interact. Once technical competence has become a given, the foundation on which successful careers are built is genuine, mutually rewarding relationships.

Look at the person at the very top of your own organization. It is unlikely that he or she is a rocket scientist or could find a cure for cancer. In fact, there are probably many people smarter, and perhaps more technically capable, than this person. Despite this lack of genius, he or she found the way to the top. It is likely due to basic competence combined with the relationships that were built throughout his or her career.

Then there are those who build good relationships—but only with those at levels in the organization that are higher than their own. It is a clever move, but a mistake in the long term. You may be able to identify people like this in your own organization. They're like heat-seeking missiles. Watch them in a room full of people—they'll gravitate toward those with the most power. The only problem is, power shifts. Those in power today may be out tomorrow.

I once worked with a woman who built her career on relationships with people in power. She managed up quite successfully, but she failed to gain the commitment of her colleagues and staff. Because of her relationships with senior management, she traded favors to become exempt from the grunt work the rest of us had to do. It worked for a while, but then, as in most corporations, the power shifted. Her protectors were out, and a new wave of power brokers swept in. The new people in power had, at one time, been the woman's colleagues. They had long memories and short tolerance for her. Within months she was looking for another job.

Fear of losing your job should not be the primary reason for building relationships with people at all levels of the organization. Throughout the organization, a wealth of information resides within the rank and file, and at some point you will have a need for it. It is a lot easier to gain access to information when you already have a relationship in place at the time you need the information than to try to do so with someone with whom you never took the time to speak in the hallway or the coffee room.

Former president Jimmy Carter is an example of someone who

prematurely derailed due to the failure to build relationships until it was too late. Carter was an "outsider" when he arrived in Washington. His blind spot with regard to the need for relationships with Congress was only amplified when he appointed fellow Georgians, with little political experience, to key positions in the White House. Carter lacked fundamental knowledge of how Washington really works. He is an example of someone who won the election because of the appeal of a particular strength, which was not being a part of the established Washington scene, but who ultimately failed because he did not complement this strength with new behaviors. He had few "chips" in his bank account when it came to relationships with Congress, and this made it difficult for him to implement an effective domestic policy during his one-term presidency. It is little wonder that his greatest achievements, both then and now, are *outside* the borders of the United States. Carter's legacy will forever be the international relationships he forged, not his domestic ones.

Once you have achieved technical competence, building relationships is the most important thing that you can do to continue your success and avoid derailment. *How do you do it?* Those people who received more reinforcement for task accomplishment than for relationship building initially in their careers won't find it particularly easy or comfortable. Like Diane, who was described earlier in this chapter, you may have to take some risks and be willing to stop hiding behind your technical competence. One thing is certain, the profit will outweigh the risk in the long term.

Listening with a Third Ear

When John F. Kennedy Jr. was asked what he thought his father would most like to be remembered for, he replied, "For being a good listener." Others had shared stories about how his father could make the people who spoke with him feel as though they were the only people in the world. The president's ability to concentrate singularly on the person speaking was one of the behaviors that also endeared him to others. Anne Morrow Lindbergh, author and wife of the aviator Charles Lindbergh, underscores the importance of this trait: "It is not possible to talk wholeheartedly to more than one person at a time. You can't really talk to a person unless you surrender to them for the moment (all other talk is futile). You can't surrender to more than one person a moment."

Listening is the most important thing that you can do to build, and maintain, relationships. Most people spend the greatest part of their days hearing what others say, yet few people really listen. They don't take the time to fully understand what other people think, what problems they may be encountering, or even how they might feel. There are myriad reasons why it is difficult to surrender to another, and the reasons differ from person to person. Decide which reasons on this list are *your* greatest obstacles to listening.

- **REHEARSING.** Mentally practicing what you're going to say before the speaker stops talking is rehearsing. The moment you start rehearsing, you stop listening.

- **THE HALO EFFECT.** This is thinking that you already know what someone is going to say, or putting a positive or negative slant on the message, based on your previous relationship with him or her. For example, if every time Bob comes into my office he gives me bad news, before long, when I see Bob, I cast a negative halo around all of his messages, regardless of actual content. Conversely, if Ingrid and I have a great relationship, then her messages tend to be perceived positively, no matter what the content.

- **PSEUDOLISTENING.** Pretending to listen (and even looking like you are) when in fact you're thinking about something other than the message is pseudolistening. You know that you've been busted when the speaker asks, "So what do you think?" and you don't have a clue about what he just said.

• **DISTRACTIONS.** When you are preoccupied with other thoughts or problems, you become distracted and unable to listen to the message. Also, interruptions or noise (phones ringing, people coming in and out of your office, noise from the hallway) that make it difficult to concentrate on the speaker's message are common workplace distractions.

• **LISTENING FOR A POINT OF DISAGREEMENT.** We all know people who wait for one point with which they can disagree so that they can look intelligent, one-up the speaker, or impress others in the conversation.

• **NERVOUSNESS.** Anxiety about the situation, the message, or upcoming responsibilities impedes being able to fully listen to the message.

• **DISINTEREST.** It is difficult to listen to the subject or the speaker if the topic is of no interest to you.

• **POOR SPEAKER.** A speaker who is boring, has difficulty making his or her point, or who makes the subject dry and tedious is someone to whom you may be unlikely to listen.

You will have to ascertain for yourself the reasons why you fail to completely surrender yourself to others when they speak. Once you do, you'll be able to overcome some of your difficulties by engaging in the technique of *active listening* developed by the psychologist Carl Rogers. He coined the term *unconditional positive regard* to refer to the process by which you enter into a relationship believing the best about another person. Without strings attached or qualification, you hold another person in high esteem. In order to really listen to someone, you first must have unconditional positive regard for him or her. Otherwise, the halo effect overshadows the message. Rogers said that once you have unconditional positive regard, active listening, rather than the passive taking in of information, can help you to assure that you've actually heard not only the message, but what the speaker may *not* be saying as well.

Active listening involves these three steps:

1. **PARAPHRASING.** This is the act of repeating (in your own words) what you think the speaker has just said. If you haven't really listened, then you can't do it. If you haven't surrendered yourself to the speaker, paraphrasing isn't as easy as it sounds. You need not worry about repeating the message verbatim. When you paraphrase the other person will let you know whether you have heard him or her correctly. Paraphrasing also has the secondary benefit of allowing the speaker to hear his or her message played back. After a paraphrase, it's not unusual to hear someone say, "That's what I said, but it's not what I meant." It allows clarification for both the speaker and the listener.

Here's an example of a paraphrase:

Speaker: *Whew! I'm glad that presentation is over. Every member of the board of directors was there, and every one of them had questions. What was supposed to be a fifteen-minute presentation turned into an hour of picking apart every last detail of the proposed new building site.*

Listener: *Sounds like your audience really raked you over the coals.*

Speaker: *And how. I never knew there could be so many differences of opinion about what I thought was a done deal. At least I was able to answer every question.*

When you paraphrase, the speaker feels heard and is encouraged to continue. Paraphrasing alone, however, gives the impression of simply parroting the speaker. The next step in active listening is being able to ask questions that provide for further clarification and full understanding.

2. **ASKING APPROPRIATE QUESTIONS.** By asking questions, both you and the speaker delve more deeply into the con-

tent of the message. An appropriate question is always one that is *based on what has just been said.* All too often the listener changes the direction of the conversation by asking a question unrelated to what the speaker is saying. On the surface, it may appear appropriate, but closer examination reveals that it is really just a polite way to change the subject. An example of an *inappropriate* question based on the above conversation would be, "What did you think about the guy from ABC Company? I'm going to have to meet with him next week." Active listening for the purpose of building relationships is designed to help you to hear and understand another person, not get your needs met at that particular moment.

If the listener wants to build a relationship with this speaker, then the focus has to remain with the speaker. Here's how the conversation might continue:

Listener: *Do you think the project might be stalled?*

Speaker: *Not really. It's just that everyone was trying to one-up everyone else, and the only way they could really do it was by showing how much they knew about the building site and proposal. I just got caught in the cross fire. I guess I thought that the presentation was pro forma, when in fact I see now that it was a political decision to put me on the agenda.*

Now the listener has even more information about what happened, why the speaker thinks it happened, and, without directly saying it, how he or she might feel. Here is where the third part of active listening comes in: the ability to extrapolate the speaker's feelings from the spoken message by reading between the lines.

3. **REFLECTING FEELINGS.** This is the toughest part of active listening. It involves making a guess at how you think the other person must feel. It brings the relationship to an even deeper level of understanding. People who have difficulty expressing their own feelings have difficulty with listening to and reflecting

the feelings of others. If you reflect feelings and they're ignored, or the conversation comes to a grinding halt, it's best to drop this step. Part of being an active listener and listening with a third ear includes the ability to respond to the needs of the speaker. If talking about feelings makes him or her uncomfortable, don't push. Not everyone wants his or her feelings reflected, but those who do will appreciate a well-timed reflection.

The same conversation might continue with this reflection combined with continued paraphrasing and asking questions:

Listener: *You must have felt as though you were ambushed.*

Speaker: *Yeah, I was pretty mad. I wished that someone had let me know what the real agenda was instead of my having to figure it out for myself. I guess I felt a little foolish.*

Listener: *I don't blame you for feeling as you do. What are you going to do about it?*

Speaker: *I'm not sure yet. I do know that I don't want to be put in that situation again—or at least I want to be forewarned about it.*

Listener: *How do you think you might prevent it from happening in the future?*

Speaker: *I guess I should talk to the boss. She's usually open to hearing me out. I think I'll sleep on it and decide tomorrow what to do.*

Listener: *Sounds like a good idea. Let me know if I can help in any way.*

Speaker: *You already have.*

This conversation could have gone in any number of directions—and all away from the speaker's feelings. Active listening helps you to stay focused on the topic and not be distracted by tangential issues or personal needs. As you can see, it requires surrendering to the speaker and putting your own opinion on hold for the moment. The speaker walks away feeling as if he or she has really been heard, and the listener benefits from understanding the full context of the message—both content and emotion.

Using Doorway Conversations to Build Relationships

Now that you know how to listen, the next question is, to what degree are you comfortable taking the time to do it? If relationships are the cornerstone of ongoing career success, then doorway conversations are the cornerstone of relationships. The term *doorway conversations* comes from a client who uses it to describe those moments when someone appears in your doorway and stands there talking about the latest headline, the previous night's baseball game, or a problem he or she is encountering with a child. In the scheme of things, it may seem trivial to spend time talking about these subjects, but in the long term, these are the very things on which relationships are built. As Dale Carnegie once said, "You can make more friends in two months by becoming interested in other people than you can in two years by trying to get other people interested in you."

Relationships that are valuable and meaningful have three essential ingredients: trust, reciprocity, and genuine caring. There's no faking these three elements. They are what distinguish a casual encounter from a real relationship. This is not to say that every workplace relationship must be of the same caliber as the relationships you have with your best friends, but rather that both relationships share common elements. People who fail to build solid workplace relationships are frequently the same ones who fail to build solid friendships. The same childhood defense mechanisms get in the way of both growing close to a friend and knowing a colleague on more than a superficial level. People who have no trouble building relationships may at this point be saying, But all of this is so obvious! It may be obvious for you, but for people who have never built mutually rewarding relationships, especially in the workplace, the next section is critical.

Trust

How do you develop trust? Why do we trust some people more than others? Why are certain people everyone's trusted friend whereas others have difficulty getting people to confide in them? The answer lies in the degree to which you act consistently and honestly. Consistency is the key to enabling others to know what to expect from you. Honesty lets them know that you do what you say you will. Combined, these qualities are very powerful in building trust in the workplace.

One of the more bizarre cases that I investigated when I was an equal employment opportunity specialist involved a woman who filed a sex discrimination charge with the California Department of Fair Employment and Housing claiming that her boss was rude, condescending, and treated her unfairly. She believed that this was because she was a woman and that the men in her department were not treated similarly. In interviewing both male and female coworkers it turned out that they did not share her opinion that women were treated unfairly, and, in fact, they trusted their boss very much. How could there be such disparate opinions of the same boss? Each of the people interviewed admitted that the boss was difficult and could be rude and obnoxious. He would yell at them in front of colleagues and embarrass them at meetings, but they watched him do this to everyone, not any one individual. "It's just the way he is" was a common remark.

The irony in this situation was that they trusted him because he acted consistently and honestly with everyone. They knew exactly what to expect from him, even if it was inappropriate behavior, and therefore always knew where they stood. Winning this case for the company relied on men in the department being willing to state that they were treated the same as the woman filing the claim. There was no unlawful discrimination—just poor management, which is exactly what the commission eventually determined.

It is not recommended that you show everyone the same terrible treatment that this man did, but there is a lesson here. Even in the face of adversity, people will trust if there is consistency. Now, imagine the kind of trusting relationships that could be built with *positive* behaviors! Think of the people that you trust. It is likely that you're willing to go the extra mile for them because you know that they are true to their words.

Reciprocity

Reciprocity involves not only the quid pro quo exchanges described earlier in this chapter, but also a mutuality of sharing. In a solid workplace relationship, each person knows that the other has similar feelings about the nature of the friendship. They know this because there is a mutual sharing of personal information, allowing the "human side" to emerge. Too many of us have been taught that there's no place at work for personal problems or personal information to be shared. However, because we spend the largest part of our day at work it is only natural to disclose personal information in the workplace. In instances in which a person may be a good listener but does not share personal information, that person will soon set himself or herself apart from everyone else.

Adults who come from narcissistic parents are particularly vulnerable to this dilemma. They learned early in life that they are merely reflections of their parents and, therefore, should not think that their own needs deserve consideration. They go through life listening, but not telling. In a workplace relationship, the person who is always doing the talking may begin to feel uncomfortable about continuing to share information when he or she knows nothing about the other person in return. In reality, it takes very little self-disclosure to create a sense of mutuality. It must simply be enough to illuminate the human side of your character.

Recently at a workshop that I was conducting, I mentioned a personal experience that demonstrated the need for paraphrasing and asking questions when engaged in a conversation. I remarked that I had initially misunderstood the person with whom I had been collaborating about the program design and had, therefore, wasted quite a bit of time designing the wrong program. After the program a woman came up to me and, somewhat critically, asked why I had the need to make myself look bad in front of the group. She felt that the comment was unnecessary. I explained that I want program participants to see me as human and that the comment was a quite intentional way to accomplish this.

Often, as with the woman mentioned above, the fear that people have that they will be seen as less competent or somehow imperfect precludes them from being genuine with others. However, honest self-disclosure can be a valuable tool in letting others see the human side of you, and most people do not take advantage of it. The willingness to be seen and heard can be quite a liberating experience.

Genuine Caring

The last of the three ingredients for successful relationships, genuine caring, is the hardest of all to coach. It is something that comes from deep inside the heart and transcends logic and intellect. The absence of caring is a lot easier to explain than how to care, because the absence suggests the lack of caring in one's own life. With the exception of perhaps sociopaths, who truly lack the ability to care about their fellow human beings, most people have a deep and profound capacity to care. Women tend to have an easier time showing that they care, but it doesn't mean that men don't. Men have simply been socialized to hide it better. Therefore, the question is not "How can I show that I care?" but rather, "Why *don't* I show that I care?" When you have the answer to this, you'll have the answer for how to genuinely care.

Chris, a woman I had coached, appeared not to care at all about her staff of twenty salespeople. Chris's single-minded devotion was to provide the best service possible to the company's customers. Her natural energy and enthusiasm made her want to take every hill that she encountered. She was always coming up with unique and creative ways to better serve the customer and overcome existing obstacles to superior service. There is nothing wrong with that, but Chris failed to take into account the fact that she could successfully do this only if her staff followed her into battle. While Chris was charging up the hill, she failed to look behind her and see that her followers were lingering at the bottom, deciding whether or not to take the hill.

My first contact with Chris was through a team-building session that she requested to find ways for her staff to be more effective. When it came time to assess the team's strengths and developmental areas, the primary complaint of her staff was that Chris didn't care about them—she was so self-absorbed that she didn't care whether or not her staff had the time, resources, and interest in pursuing the projects to which she committed them. So, when it came time to deliver, Chris was often left holding the bag and trying to figure out why. Chris neglected the human needs of her team, and they responded (very humanly) by resisting her efforts.

Chris was hired because it was clear that she could bring value-added service to this company. Her past achievements in former employment situations pointed to this fact. Chris saw herself as someone who could do anything she put her mind to, and she typically did, provided that she could do it alone. When it came to gaining the cooperation of others, she couldn't quite figure out why she never really got it. Heretofore, Chris had been a tremendous individual contributor, but in order to avoid career derailment she was at the point in her career where she had to learn how to accomplish the goal through others.

Fortunately for this team, Chris did care about other people. She just had a hard time showing it. Chris told me about her military father who expected high achievement but seldom rewarded it. She realized that, in some ways, she had become her father. She expected a lot from her team, but she didn't see them as people, only as objects there to assist her with meeting her goals. When she understood how this behavior impeded her reaching the goal, she was actually distraught. She had vowed never to do to others what her father had done to her and yet now she found that she was displaying the same behavior. Chris had to learn to complement her already good task-oriented behaviors with skills for building relationships with each team member and creating a cohesive team. Chris was able to draw on her teenage experience as a member of a tennis team to remind her of the value of teamwork. It was helpful because she had a point of reference for just how interdependence works.

Chris began with doorway conversations—just dropping by to say hello to people and to find out how—not what—they were doing. At first, they regarded her with skepticism. They wondered what ulterior motives she had. This discouraged Chris initially, but she was determined to win them over. She approached building relationships in much the same way as she approached her other "projects"—with vigor and enthusiasm. Pretty soon the individuals on her team began responding to her friendly overtures and expressions of interest. Chris didn't do it to get more work out of her team, but to get to know them as unique and valuable individuals. Chris learned the true meaning of Chinese philosopher Lao-tzu's saying "Fail to honor people, they fail to honor you." It took Chris a while, but she finally succeeded in building trust, reciprocity, and caring into workplace relationships. That's what made team members work for Chris in the long term and helped her to avoid premature career derailment.

Empathy

Empathy is a bit like caring. It is pretty tough to teach someone to be empathetic, but it is another important aspect of building relationships. If you can't empathize with someone, you can't really understand them. Empathy is the ability to put yourself in the other person's shoes and feel what they feel. It differs from sympathy in that sympathy requires only that you be able to see intellectually what another person is experiencing, not necessarily understand how that person feels. Sympathy is a more cognitive process, whereas empathy is a more emotional one.

I am not even sure that I would have thought to include the importance of empathy in relationship building had I not taken the time to have a conversation with a wonderful program administrator named Andrew. As we were both waiting for participants to arrive at a one-week program being held in Prague, we discussed what made certain programs go well and others not so well for him as an administrator. He remarked that it really made a difference when participants could *empathize* with how difficult it was to respond to their requests in the exact time frame that they wanted. As a program administrator, his responsibility involves taking care of all of the little details that participants might require. This includes making flight arrangements, ordering special meals, scheduling ground transportation, sending or receiving faxes, and making dinner reservations. The comment that really got my attention was, "When people show a little empathy I'll go the extra mile. When they treat me as though I have no brains, I act as though I have no brains."

It was one of those *aha!* moments. Part of the quid pro quo involves understanding what it's like to be in another person's position. Not looking simply at the job, but at the person in the job as well—seeing the human being performing the task. It made sense. Treating someone impersonally, like a functionary, does little to secure the relationship and assure longer-term cooperation.

What does it take to be empathetic? It takes surrender, in much the same way as Anne Morrow Lindbergh described it. It takes a suspension of personal need, judgment, or urgency in an effort to connect with the person with whom you are interacting. Empathy is what is missing from sociopaths—they cannot relate in any way to the victim. Those criminals who commit brutal murders and feel no remorse lack empathy. Those people who cry when they see pictures of the atrocities of war have empathy. Empathy in the workplace is exhibited by noticing, and commenting on, changes in mood or behavior, by talking about problems that may be inherent to a particular position, by following up on personal problems that may have been discussed in a passing moment. Empathy is one way of showing that (1) you care and (2) you understand.

You Like Me! You Really Like Me!

The "You Like Me" acceptance speech that Sally Field made when she won an Academy Award a number of years ago speaks to a unique issue in building relationships. It reveals why she was typically cast in "cute" roles rather than more mature ones. She had an inordinate need to be liked and that need was typified over and over in her behavior. So, a word of caution about building positive relationships: There is a difference between taking the time to build positive relationships and making it the focal point of every day because you're afraid people won't like you. An inordinate need to be liked interferes with your ability to make difficult decisions, be direct with people, get your own needs met, and be perceived as someone who can perform even when the chips are down.

Although both men and women suffer from this problem, it seems to be more prevalent among women—and for good reason. Women have been socialized to be the nurturers, caretakers, and accommodators in society. They are expected to be good relationship builders. When women act in a manner counter to that expectation, they are often called overly aggressive, bitchy, or some other choice terms. So, they go out of their way to be pleasant and try to win support for their ideas by making others like them. Overutilization of this particular strength can create situations where others don't take you seriously. Ironically, it is the people, both men and women, who have established good workplace relationships who can well afford to err on the side of being more assertive or direct. Their accounts are full of chips that can be used at the appropriate time.

Maria is a good example of someone whose strength in building relationships interfered with her ability to achieve her career goals. She is the coordinator of outreach efforts for a nonprofit organization. Technically, she knows her job and is respected for her ability to perform it effectively. But when the department manager position has opened up on several occasions, she has consistently been overlooked as a viable candidate to fill it. When she has asked why, she has been told that she "isn't ready" to take this next step.

If you were to meet Maria, you would like her—as does everyone in her office. She's warm, affable, and a good listener. She makes you feel as if what you have to say is important to her. If you spend any length of time with her, however, you realize that her strength in this arena stems from the need to be liked and is not balanced with the ability to be direct and straightforward. If she has an opinion different from yours, she won't tell you. She'll embrace yours as if it were her own. She won't take a stand on any issue if she thinks it might offend you. If you correct something that she does wrong, she becomes overly apologetic and tries to make up for the mistake by bringing you home-baked cookies the next day. Maria will never be considered "management material" until she overcomes this particular strength by balancing it with more assertive behaviors.

It is understood that relationships will never take the place of technical competence; they complement and support it. The ability to see and be seen is an essential ingredient for all good relationships, workplace and otherwise. One method by which you can avoid premature career derailment is by balancing excellence in technical capability with building one-on-one relationships that help you to achieve your goals through cooperation and camaraderie.

Beyond making an individual contribution and building one-on-one relationships, you have to work effectively as part of a team. The next chapter provides suggestions for how you can be an effective team member and contribute to your team's success.

Ways to Build Strong One-On-One Relationships

1. At least once a week have lunch with one or more coworkers.
2. Drop into one person's office per day for ten minutes of casual conversation.
3. Smile at people as you walk past them in the hall.
4. Have your desk situated so that it faces out the door.
5. Keep your office door open unless you are conducting confidential business or trying to meet a tight deadline and don't want distractions (but never more than a few times each month).
6. When people talk to you, surrender yourself for the moment.
7. Open up to people to let them get to know you by disclosing personal information with which you are comfortable.
8. Read *People Skills: How to Assert Yourself, Listen to Others, and Resolve Conflicts* (see page 247).

9. Solicit input from knowledgeable coworkers about projects on which you are working.

10. Accept coworkers' invitations for lunch or dinner and extend your own.

11. Attend company-sponsored social events.

12. Learn the names of coworkers' husbands, wives, significant others, and children.

13. Remember birthdays by keeping a list or marking them on your calendar.

14. Follow up on information that has been previously shared with you, particularly personal information.

15. Learn the names of everyone on your floor and in the departments with which you interact most frequently.

16. Say thank you when someone goes out of the way for you.

17. Go out of your way for others.

18. Interact with everyone equally, regardless of level in the organization.

19. Begin conversations with small talk, unless you know the other person doesn't like it.

20. Enroll in The Dale Carnegie Course (see page 239).

21. Don't allow an inordinate need for others to like you to get in the way of being direct and straightforward.

22. Put yourself in the shoes of the other person.

23. Do favors for people even if you don't anticipate needing them returned.

24. See beyond the task to the human being who is performing it.

Inability to Function Effectively in a Work Group

BECOME AN INTEGRAL MEMBER OF YOUR TEAM

One by-product of building relationships is the often unexpected, but always welcomed, gift of insight provided by those who have a view of the world that is different from my own. For example, toward the end of a meeting with my client and friend Ben Hunter, controller of payroll and compensation accounting at the consulting firm McKinsey & Company, he casually inquired into what new and exciting things I was doing lately. I told him about this book, and we began discussing what made successful people derail. I happened to mention that I had decided to discuss interpersonal and team relationships in one chapter rather than discussing them separately. Ben seemed surprised. He thought that the skills required to build relationships with individuals were quite different from those used to work as an integral member of a team and deserved independent attention. We didn't have time for an in-depth discussion about it, but his comments remained with me long after our meeting ended.

As I continued thinking about it, I realized that Ben was right. I have encountered people who were terrific team players, but who were unable to forge deeper, more intimate, one-on-one relationships. Teamwork allows for anonymity, depending on the size of groups, but effective interpersonal relationships do not. It is easier to "hide" personally in a group than it is in individual relationships, provided you contribute to task accomplishment.

Conversely, people who create strong personal support systems consisting of relationships with individuals may derail due to their inability to participate as members of task forces or project teams. Their discomfort with groups precludes them from making the same contribution to a team that they might when working independently or with just one other person on a project. These people do quite well one-on-one, but somehow become lost in a group.

So, I would like to thank Ben for his insight. The ability to work effectively as a team member is not simply an extension of good interpersonal skills, but a separate and unique skill set.

Even if building relationships is one of your strengths, this checklist might reveal a very different area for potential derailment.

_____ I would describe myself as a good team player.

_____ Even when the topic doesn't interest me, isn't pertinent to my function, or I have nothing to add, I stay engaged in team discussions by looking for ways to contribute to the outcome.

_____ I believe that the final product of a group typically exceeds the quality of something that I produce alone.

_____ I freely share information with teammates without questioning their "need to know."

_____ I believe that differences of opinion on a team add value to, rather than simply delay, outcomes.

_____ I understand the difference between the task and the process of a team.

_____ I am comfortable with being a follower while someone else leads a group.

_____ I do not display impatience with the lengthy discussions that are often part of a group's process because I know that they will contribute positively to the outcome.

_____ I volunteer for team-based projects.

_____ Getting individual recognition is not as important to me as my team's success.

_____ I publicly acknowledge others who have worked with me on a successful project.

The Value of Teamwork

Because most cultures reward competition and individualism with money and recognition, there are those who question the value of developing cooperative team abilities. Some people prefer to be "individual contributors" and in fact work more effectively in this way. They tend to avoid opportunities to work collaboratively. The efficacy of teamwork, however, is well documented through sports analogies, war and peace efforts, and medical triage. The following routine training exercise for flight attendants underscores the importance and value of teamwork.

When flight attendants are trained in techniques for aircraft crash survival at sea, they are taught to look for passengers at the beginning of a flight who are most likely to survive on a raft and contribute to the survival of others. The key to ensuring successful survival is in choosing people who can play all kinds of roles at sea. A leader is needed who can remind others of the vision of being rescued. He or she can keep people optimistic about their chances of staying alive by remaining calm, having faith in and seeing the "big picture," whether this is called faith in God or a higher power. Beyond this role, technical competence is required to survive as well—to desalinate saltwater, repair a tear in the raft, read a compass, or administer first aid. In the end, survival depends not on any single skill set, but rather on taking advantage of the fact that the whole is greater than the sum of the parts. The chance of survival increases with the synergistic effect of teamwork. Paradoxically, as people pool their resources, instead of focusing exclusively on their own survival, the likelihood of success increases exponentially.

The same is true in organizations. Individuals come to the workplace with unique skill sets that contribute to their own success and the success of their teams. Each of us is endowed with things that we do well and for which people rely on us. Some of these skills are learned, others are developed with practice, and still others are the result of our natural proclivity for them. We aren't expected to do everything equally well, but we are expected to use the resources around us, including the human resources, to accomplish our tasks effectively. Much like the survivors of an airplane crash, business survivors must have the ability to perform tasks not only independently or together with only one other person, but collaboratively in group settings as well.

Team-based projects have become increasingly popular and appear to be here to stay. It is important that you be able to work effectively not only with individuals, but also with entire teams of people. Whereas some people are able to forge good one-on-one workplace relationships, others excel and find satisfaction in participating as members of a group committed to a common goal.

The term *good individual contributor* refers to someone who does his or her job well working independently, but doesn't function effectively as a member of a team. The term is frequently used to describe someone with good technical skills but poor interpersonal ones, so don't take it as a compliment if someone tells you that you're a terrific individual contributor. The message may be that you are not perceived as a good team player. Even jobs that appear on the surface to be perfect for individual contributors later turn out to be ones that require integrated teamwork. As a matter of fact, it is difficult to think of one job in most workplaces today that doesn't require integrated teamwork. Teams accomplish significantly more through the synergistic process of sharing information, technology, or skills than would a group of individual contributors working on pieces of the same project.

The experience of one major car manufacturer is testament to this fact. The company traditionally put people into assembly-line jobs where each worker was responsible for one part of the car. The frequent occurrence of production mistakes forced management to examine the inefficiency and find ways of overcoming it. The managers discovered that by increasing the scope of each person's position and creating teams of people who had overall responsibility for the car's assembly rather than each person being responsible for only one piece, the quality of the automobiles produced actually increased.

In a different kind of business, the Ritz-Carlton hotel chain also stresses teamwork in addition to excellence in individual performance during new employee orientation at each facility. A stay at any one of the hotels is likely to make you realize that the Ritz-Carlton has redefined *customer service* in the broadest sense of the term. Each employee is taught that he or she is personally responsible for the satisfaction of the hotel's guests. Employees are not taught to do just one job well; they are taught to work as a part of the overall hotel team of staff members and to accept responsibility for *any* request that a guest might make.

During a leadership workshop at the Ritz-Carlton in Pasadena, California, the cofacilitator of the program decided to test the hotel's philosophy to see whether it worked in practice. Several times during our stay, she would ask staff members for items or services that were clearly outside the domain of their responsibility. Each time her request was promptly met. In an effort to make a point to the managers in this workshop about the value of teamwork, she asked a man from the catering staff, who came in to refresh the coffee, whether he knew where we could get some masking tape. He said that he would take care of it. Several minutes later he returned, masking tape in hand.

After she thanked him, I asked how he liked working at this hotel. He said that it was one of the best jobs that he ever had. When I asked why, he said because he was trained to do his job properly *and* felt like an important part of the hotel team. He said that each morning management held team meetings to talk about the guests and their particular needs so that *everyone* would have all of the information required to meet the demands. It was a valuable lesson to the participants about the efficacy of teamwork and how it can enhance customer *and* employee satisfaction.

Another example of the value of teamwork is provided by the relatively new restaurant chain California Pizza Kitchens. With a main fare of individual gourmet pizza and pasta, the restaurants first opened in California in the late 1980s. Since that time they have grown significantly and have expanded to several states across the country. Besides serving good food (showing that they are technically competent), these restaurants also offer a pleasant dining experience. Their waiters and waitresses have been trained in how to treat customers and how to work as a team. There are no fixed table assignments for servers—everyone is responsible for every table. When I inquired how this worked with regard to tips, I was told by one young man that it wasn't a problem. Peer pressure essentially eliminated those staff people who brought down the tip average for the others.

An example of effective teamwork that supersedes individual team member differences can be seen among the group of lawyers assembled for what the media has proclaimed the trial of the cen-

tury: *The People of the State of California v. Orenthal James Simpson.*
Simpson, given his years as a professional football player, knew the
value of teamwork. He was represented by a defense team on
which each lawyer was, in his own right, an outstanding individual contributor but could probably not have alone saved Simpson
from being convicted. Together, they successfully defended Simpson and helped him to avoid what would in all likelihood have
been years in prison.

It wasn't until after the trial was over that the public became
aware of the strong feelings of antagonism among the team members. Attorney Robert Shapiro went so far as to say that he would
never again work with at least one of his trial colleagues, and similar insinuations were made by many of the key players. The outcome of the trial speaks loudly to the ability of individuals to put
aside their differences for the purpose of achieving a common goal
in an uncommon manner.

Perhaps the sports arena offers the greatest source for understanding the importance of teamwork. Sports teams consist of
groups of outstanding individual contributors who know that
they can't win the game alone—and if they think they can, they
don't get the cooperation of their teammates for long. Chicago
Bulls head coach Phil Jackson had this lesson emphasized for him
the hard way. In his book *Sacred Hoops: Spiritual Lessons of a Hardwood Warrior,* Jackson shares an experience from an early stint as
coach with the Albany Patroons. Despite the fact that he had no
formal training as a coach, he did have a coaching vision: "to create a team in which selflessness—not the me-first mentality that
had come to dominate professional basketball—was the primary
driving force." Part of his method for accomplishing the vision
was to assure that everyone on the team be paid the same amount
and be given equal playing time.

His strategy worked. Within two years, the Patroons moved
from an 8–17 season to having the second best record in the

league, with Jackson being named Coach of the Year. His achievement began to unravel, however, when he allowed one player, Frankie J. Sanders, to dominate the game and compromise his principles. Sanders first convinced Jackson to move him from second slot to starting player, then successfully lobbied management for a sizable raise. Combined with his superior playing skill, these factors gave Sanders (and his teammates) the impression that he was first among equals. Following a series of incidents that included Jackson's suspending Sanders (for what amounted to insubordination) and then implicitly supporting management's decision to reinstate him (because they felt he was needed to win games), the team was never the same. "The solidarity that had taken so long to build had suddenly evaporated," writes Jackson. "Not only did we lose the series, we were lost as a team."

Clearly, teamwork pays huge dividends for both individuals and groups of people. Why, then, do so many people derail due to the inability to work as part of a team? The reason so many people resist teamwork lies partially in how jobs came into being in the first place.

Overcoming Resistance to Teamwork

The concept of working independently in a "job" is a relatively recent phenomenon born of the industrial revolution. It was during this period that individual jobs were created as a means of responding to the requirements imposed by factory assembly procedures. Throughout history, however, human beings worked much more collaboratively to assure their survival. Clans, tribes, and families can be viewed as the earliest teams. Even in prehistoric time, our predecessors pooled resources by allowing those with the best vision to sight their prey, those with the best dexterity to kill it, and those with the greatest strength to haul it back to the cave.

Consciously or otherwise, they realized that their survival depended on a collaborative effort.

Today, in an age where rugged individualism and an "everyone for themselves" attitude prevails, teamwork seems like a revolutionary concept. The irony is that people resist having to depend on others for their success when in fact they would fare so much better if they worked collaboratively. In their wonderfully written and enlightening book, *The Wisdom of Teams,* Jon Katzenbach and Douglas Smith recognize that there exists a natural resistance to moving from individual contributor to team player. "Our natural instincts, family upbringing, formal education, and employment experience all stress the primary importance of individual responsibility as measured by our own standards and those to whom we report," Katzenbach and Smith write. "We are more comfortable doing our own jobs and having our performance measured by our boss than we are working and jointly being assessed as peers."

The story of a man whom I met during a team-building session in Germany provides insight into how and why some people resist teamwork. Erik was raised in a small village about eighty miles outside of Berlin. Throughout the program he arrived late to each of the sessions, sat on the outside of the small groups to which he was assigned, and spoke very quietly, which led to him often being ignored, after which he would shut down completely. Combined, his behavior and body language indicated that he was resisting this team's effort to coalesce.

After one particularly intense group exercise where several members of the team received some pretty difficult feedback, Erik raised his hand and said that people never change anyway and we shouldn't expect them to. His real message being that *he* wasn't going to change. Whereas his teammates were doing their best to overcome cultural and personal obstacles to teamwork, Erik threw a monkey wrench into this painstaking process. Democracy in what was formerly East Germany is a relatively new system and the remnants of communism were reflected in the hesitance which many of the participants had in speaking openly and honestly. Erik's resistance wasn't making it any easier.

One evening I arrived late to dinner and found only Erik left at the table. We made small talk about our families and upbringing while I waited for my meal to arrive. Much to my surprise, he began telling me about his childhood with a cruel father and timid mother. In broken English, he conveyed perfectly that although his father was well intentioned (he wanted Erik to be more than the truck driver that he himself was), he was nonetheless abusive, both physically and emotionally. Erik's mother was ineffectual in preventing the damage he did to his children's psyches. As a result, he said, he always tried to do his best and worked hard to achieve his goals, never relying on anyone else for assistance.

Erik's lesson from childhood was to be strong and independent, always giving his personal best in an effort to deflect his father's constant criticism and verbal abuse. His survival, and the survival of all of the children in his family, was dependent on each person fending for him or herself. Neither could he rely on his mother, who had her own problems in the abusive atmosphere created by Erik's father. His resistance to my efforts to help this group become a high-performing team was now understandable to me. I no longer viewed Erik as an impediment to the process, but rather as a human being struggling for survival in an unknown and changing world. Erik had no idea that he now had to overcome his greatest strengths in order to assure ongoing success. It was a concept as alien to him as democracy once had been.

The ingredient essential to teamwork, trust, is missing from those most reluctant to embrace it. Somewhere along the line, they learned that they could rely only on themselves. To be a fully productive member of a team requires the ability to make a leap of faith that you will actually be better off by relinquishing some of the need to work independently. In order to do so you must first believe that other people have something valuable to offer and that together you can accomplish great things.

Understanding and Valuing "Gifts Differing"

One invaluable tool that I use in conjunction with individual coaching and team-building programs is the Myers Briggs Type Indicator (MBTI®) personality inventory. The title of a lovely companion book, *Gifts Differing,* helps us all to understand that we each bring unique gifts to the workplace. The challenge of working as part of a team is to understand the gifts that you bring *as well as* those brought by fellow team members. All too often we come to believe that the gift we bring is the *only* gift needed by the team. Success as a team member depends on your being able to value and use the gifts of others as effectively as you use your own.

The MBTI measures individual preferences on four separate scales: what energizes or takes energy away from a person, what a person likes to pay attention to, how a person makes decisions, and how a person likes to live life. On each of the four scales shown on the chart on page 72, you exhibit a preference for one set of behaviors over the other. Knowing these four things about yourself and your teammates can help you to contribute your own personal best and bring the best out in others as well. Similarly, failure to understand personality types can lead to an enormous amount of frustration and misunderstanding.

Here is an example. At a team-building session in Jakarta, Indonesia, that involved a lot of work in small groups and pairs of people, a woman, Sarinah, came up to me and whispered, "Whatever you do, don't pair me with Malu," and hurried away. Naturally, as the facilitator, this was a red flag to me that she probably *needed* to be paired with Malu. Then, a little while later, Malu came up to me and—you can already guess what she wanted—asked not to be paired with Sarinah. I was pondering how best to handle the situation when knowledge of type preferences helped me to solve this dilemma.

I typically do an exercise where people who are opposite types on the MBTI are asked to pair up together to discuss ways in which they have difficulty working as teammates and how those difficulties could be turned into opportunities. Sarinah and Malu scored as opposite profiles. Whereas Sarinah was an Extrovert / Senser / Thinker / Judger, Malu was an Introvert / Intuitor / Feeler / Perceiver. Sarinah was outgoing, practical, results-oriented, in-your-face, and Malu was more introspective, attuned to possibilities instead of reality, and sensitive to people and processes. As frequently happens when these two particular types work together without understanding how to capitalize on their differences, ongoing communication problems and misunderstandings existed between them. Malu viewed Sarinah as too blunt, unconcerned with how people felt about things, and so concerned with the bottom line that new and innovative ways of doing things were ignored. Conversely, Sarinah thought Malu was too slow to reach decisions, overly concerned with people's opinions, and withheld information.

Given my instructions, they reluctantly paired up together. Once they began talking about the problems between them based on their types, each realized that she saw the world through a different set of lenses. Instead of each thinking the other was just trying to make her life miserable, both learned that these differences could be used to help each other be more effective. As a result of their discussion they decided to use each other's strengths to complement their own and as a means of learning alternative skills. Although I don't think that Malu and Sarinah will ever be best friends, they did begin to work more effectively as teammates and overcome the barriers that existed to a collaborative working relationship.

Herein lies one of the secrets to being a successful team player: the ability to move outside the scope of your own preferences and limited worldview to a broader understanding of the complementary nature of team relationships. We get so stuck in our own paradigms that we fail to see how other paradigms add value. *Our* way of doing things becomes *the* way, thereby limiting the possibilities that result from synergistic teamwork. And the more we learned in childhood that we had to be staunchly independent and self-sufficient, the harder it is to shift our paradigms.

The importance of being able to shift paradigms is made abundantly clear in the works of the futurist Joel Barker. His book, *Paradigms: The Business of Discovering the Future,* and his film, *The Business of Paradigms,* provide examples of how the failure to move from your own comfort zone to a new, different, and perhaps unexplored sphere of possibilities can limit your future and sabotage your success. I like to tell the story of one Thanksgiving when I learned a lesson about shifting paradigms and teamwork.

It was the first year that I decided to invite a large group of relatives and friends for Thanksgiving dinner. Being the independent woman that I am, I wanted to prepare and serve the meal by myself. As more people came into the kitchen to help, I became increasingly frustrated with my inability to maintain control of the situation. My mother was telling me to do one thing to the turkey, a friend was telling me to do another to the stuffing, and still someone else was telling me how to cook the vegetables. Finally, heeding my own guidance to others that the paradox of control is *the more control you have the more you give away,* I decided to let everyone do what they wanted. I was just positive, however, that this meal would wind up a disaster.

When we finally sat down to dinner I held my breath. I would assume no responsibility for how the food tasted. No one was more surprised than I was when it turned out to be one of the best Thanksgiving dinners ever to come out of my kitchen. Too many

MBTI® PREFERENCES CHART

ENERGIZING (HOW A PERSON IS ENERGIZED)

EXTROVERT (E)	INTROVERT (I)
external	internal
outside thrust	inside pull
blurt it out	keep it in
breadth	depth
involved with people, things	work with ideas, thoughts
interaction	concentration
action	reflection
do-think-do	think-do-think

ATTENDING (WHAT A PERSON PAYS ATTENTION TO)

SENSING (S)	INTUITION (N)
the five senses	sixth sense, hunches
what is real	what could be
practical	theoretical
present orientation	future possibilities
facts	insights
using established skills	learning new skills
utility	novelty
step-by-step	leap around

DECIDING (HOW A PERSON DECIDES)

THINKING (T)	FEELING (F)
head	heart
logical system	value system
objective	subjective
justice	mercy
critique	compliment
principles	harmony
reason	empathy
firm but fair	compassionate

LIVING (LIFESTYLE A PERSON ADOPTS)	
JUDGMENT (J)	PERCEPTION (P)
planful	spontaneous
regulate	flow
control	adapt
settled	tentative
run one's life	let life happen
set goals	gather information
decisive	open
organized	flexible

Copyright © 1990 by Consulting Psychologists Press, Inc.

cooks hadn't spoiled the meal, they had made it even better than I would have done alone. There was no better way for me personally to learn the lesson that I already knew to be true for professional teams—collaboration yields a better product if you only allow the process to flow. In retrospect I realized that my resistance to teamwork in the kitchen was no different from the resistance to teamwork in the workplace. Each person came with skills different from mine, but complementary. If I had been smarter from the beginning, I would have used those skills to my advantage, rather than resisting them.

It's been more than twenty years since Chicago Bulls coach Phil Jackson vowed to trust his instincts when it comes to teamwork. During that time he's used Zen philosophy to hone his techniques for convincing individual team members about the importance and value of teamwork. In the process, he's become one of the most successful coaches in the history of the National Basketball Association. In a December 1995 interview with *Fortune* magazine he explains his approach:

> *Back in the late eighties I used to remind Michael Jordan that no matter how many great scoring games he had, he still*

*sometimes ended up coming out on the losing end, because he
would try to beat the other team by himself. Even though he could
pull it off occasionally, we weren't going to win consistently until the other players on our team started helping us. . . . Even for
people who don't consider themselves spiritual in a traditional,
religious way, you need to convince them that creating any kind
of team is a spiritual act. People have to surrender their own egos
so that the end result is bigger than the sum of its parts.*

And Jackson is right. Once you realize that you can't possibly
do it all yourself, you can begin to reap the benefits that come
from teamwork. Although you may be able to win a few games
alone, long-term wins come from interdependent team functioning, not grandstanding. It is a leap of faith to move from individual contributor to team member, but one well worth the risk.

Team Roles

Individuals must play certain roles for a sports team or a business
team to achieve its goals. The difference is that in business, groups
work on two fundamental levels: the content level and the process
level. The content level consists of the actual purpose of *what* the
group is supposed to accomplish or what goals it must achieve in
order to fulfill the expectations of management. The process level
involves *how* the group achieves those goals—something which is
frequently of lesser concern to management, but nonetheless important. Groups that focus exclusively on content get the job done,
but at a great personal cost to team members. Groups that focus exclusively on process assure that team members' personal needs are
attended to, but often at the expense of achieving their goals.

In addition to capitalizing on the gifts brought to the team by
individuals, team members must fill certain roles if the content and
the process are to be addressed. These roles are commonly divided

into two categories, which parallel the content and process of a group: task roles and group-building and maintenance roles. Whereas task roles help the group to achieve the goals expected of them, process roles are designed to maintain the emotional health of the team so that it can function effectively over the long term. Both roles are equally important, but group-building and maintenance roles are frequently ignored in favor of task accomplishment.

Task roles include behaviors such as assuring that enough information is available to make a decision, analyzing and assessing that information, rendering opinions, and moving the group toward making a decision. Most people are fairly good at playing task roles. Teams begin to encounter problems, however, when members become so focused on the task at hand that they fail to see the ramifications of their behavior on fellow teammates. They ignore the importance of maintaining relationships in group settings. You can put a really good relationship builder into a group setting and the skills he or she is comfortably able to use one-on-one go out the window. Suddenly you see counterproductive behaviors such as competitiveness, jockeying for position, talking over people, ignoring the opinions of others, and even mentally checking out when it appears the group is going in a direction different from the direction desired. Depending on one's childhood family, it may look very much like what happened at the dinner table.

One man was sent to an interpersonal skills program because he was disruptive at team meetings, always creating more turmoil than necessary, and interfering with the team's ability to reach consensus. After a videotaped exercise where he received feedback about the specific behaviors that were contributing to potential derailment, he explained why he acted as he did. He said that both of his parents were attorneys and that arguments at the dinner table were thought of as sport. His brothers and sisters, in an effort to get parental approval, would routinely take contrary positions and shout over one another in order to "win" the argument. To an outsider, he said, it would look quite bizarre. He considered chaotic team meetings the norm and actually fun. If there wasn't controversy to begin with, he created it.

Here's where team-building and maintenance roles come in. Such roles include behaviors like gatekeeping (making certain everyone is heard before the decision is made), encouraging the team to work through difficult issues, mediating differences of opinion, and relieving tension through jokes or attempts at levity. High-functioning teams assure that equal attention is paid to the team's process and its product. Failure to do so results in hard feelings among team members, outcomes being delayed, sabotage of the ultimate decision (especially when it's made by just a few group members), and the eventual dropping out of team members with valuable input.

Team-building and maintenance roles, so called because they are designed to maintain the life of the group, are more subtle, but nonetheless critical for long-term effective team functioning. If a group of people were to come together to make only one decision or complete one task and then disband and never have to work together again, the group's dynamics would be irrelevant. Exclusive focus on the task might be appropriate. In the workplace, however, individuals move from team to team and project to project, thereby necessitating assurance that each time a group meets it will successfully carry out its explicit and implicit agenda, unhampered by past or present inappropriate individual and group behavior.

During team-building sessions, I've watched as certain members become increasingly uninvolved with the team activity. They look out the window, get up and leave the room (always for a good reason, of course), or engage in pseudolistening. When asked why they mentally "checked out," they frequently respond that they didn't have anything to add or that they didn't know enough about the subject to make a contribution. This is all well and good, except for the fact that people notice when members drop out, even if they don't say anything at the moment, and the team is no longer a team. Managers who observe the process often make a mental note of who furthers goal attainment and who hinders it from lack of participation. These observations are later used as a basis for making employment decisions.

As an effective team member your job is to decide which role you are comfortable playing, or which one needs to be filled in order for the team to move forward, and to fill that role for your team. Think of yourself as a facilitator, not simply an individual contributor. Even when team meetings have a designated leader, you can help the team to meet its goals by observing the process and filling in missing roles. For example, if it seems as if the team is becoming increasingly frustrated with its inability to overcome an impasse, you can make an observation about the current climate of the group with a comment such as, "It looks as though we've reached an impasse. Let's take a minute to make sure everyone's point has been heard and understood." On the other hand, if the team is so concerned with hurting one another's feelings that decisions are being avoided, you can say something like, "It seems as though we're being very careful with one another. I'm wondering how we can make it safe enough to speak our minds without damaging any relationships."

The role of facilitator is an especially good one to play if you don't have the technical expertise required to add value to a team project or help solve a team problem. Don't wait for the formal leader of the team to take that role; at times he or she is not particularly adept at being a facilitator and your intervention will be welcomed. If you are not quite comfortable with what may appear to be usurping his or her authority, you can say, "Since this isn't my area of expertise, perhaps I could facilitate the discussion so that those of you with the knowledge can fully participate?" Playing group-building and maintenance roles keeps you connected with the team's process, makes you clearly involved to anyone who may be observing your behavior, and enables you to help your team to accomplish its goals.

People who successfully remain on their career tracks aren't the ones checking out. They know that they can always fill group-building and maintenance roles if the subject area either isn't of interest to them or isn't their forte. By shifting roles, you stay involved with the process and help the team to meet its goals by facilitating the group's activities. For example, if you become lost on the technical aspects of some discussion, look around the room and watch what is happening with the team's dynamics. Become an observer of the event itself. Check to see whether anyone else appears confused as well. If so, you can always help the team by saying something like, "It seems to me that a number of us need more explanation before we can get on board." Or, if an argument is taking place, act as mediator by interjecting, "Clearly, there's a difference of opinion. Let's see if we can reach a mutual agreement before our time is up."

Being able to build one-on-one relationships and working as part of a team are two of the most important things that you will do to assure career longevity. They'll never take the place of hard work and technical competence, but they will complement these two performance givens. If you tend to work independently, find ways to collaborate on team projects and make contributions to team meetings. Although the ability to work independently can be viewed as a strength, it must be balanced with adding value to your team and teammates.

S trategies for Team Meetings

1. Stay involved in team meetings by consciously choosing the role that you will play.

2. Act as a facilitator at team meetings.

3. Pay as close attention to the team's process as you do to achieving the task.

4. Notice and invite quieter or more reluctant members of the team to speak up.

5. Before team meetings adjourn, assure buy-in by asking whether everyone agrees with whatever decisions have been made—and if they don't, revisit the issue or schedule it for discussion at the next meeting.

6. Suggest that the last fifteen minutes of team meetings be used to talk about the team's process and what could be done differently at the next meeting to make it more productive.

7. Stay tuned in when the meeting topic isn't immediately applicable to your present work by looking for the opportunity to learn something new that may be useful to you later.

S trategies to Use Between Meetings

8. Volunteer for projects that require you to work with at least two other people.

9. Be willing to give up your way of doing things if it means the team will benefit.

10. Rather than seeing differences of opinion as obstacles, use them to reach well-rounded solutions to team problems.

11. Circulate articles that you think may be of interest to teammates.

12. Showcase the accomplishments of teammates as well as your own.

13. Move from "me" to "we" thinking.

14. Share information freely without considering whether there is the need to know.

15. Ask teammates for input into projects for which you have primary responsibility.

16. Suggest celebrating team accomplishments with a small party, public recognition, time off, token gifts, etc.

17. Volunteer to help teammates who may be under a tight deadline or experiencing a time crunch.

18. Don't be afraid to ask for help when you are experiencing a time crunch.

P ersonal Development

19. Take a class in group dynamics.
20. Read *Please Understand Me* (see page 247).
21. Critically assess your behavior on teams and make adjustments as needed.
22. Instead of viewing other people's strengths as a threat, use them to complement your own.
23. Read *Mining Group Gold* (see page 247).
24. Read *The Wisdom of Teams* (see page 249)

Failure to Focus on Image and Communication

CAPITALIZE ON THE POWER OF PERCEPTION

In 1995, for nearly a full year, the world was mesmerized by a real-life courtroom drama called *The People of the State of California v. Orenthal James Simpson*. Although many of the players on that legal stage provide us with tremendous insight into the power of perception as it relates to credibility, perhaps no two players illustrate the counterpoint more effectively than prosecutor Christopher Darden and defense attorney Johnnie Cochran. From the beginning of the trial we knew that only one of the men could prevail in his quest for justice, but we may not have realized that it would at least partially hinge on factors related to image and communication: the ability to convince a jury that he alone spoke the truth.

Both Darden and Cochran are well educated, intelligent, and articulate men. They worked hard for the career success they have achieved. In many ways they can be considered equals in the legal arena. One major difference between them, however, is their communication styles—and soon after the trial began the courtroom camera captured these differences. As Darden became frustrated with the tactics of his opponents, viewers could see and hear the change in his demeanor. He became increasingly sullen and morose. He questioned witnesses in such a low tone of voice that it was often difficult to hear him. He appeared lethargic and, at times, indifferent to the court proceedings. Sarcastic remarks and disparaging facial expressions bespoke his contempt for the court, his opponents, and the defendant. In short, Darden looked and sounded like a man defeated before the final bell.

On the other hand, with few exceptions, Cochran presented the picture of composure throughout the trial. He would vehemently argue his points, but when decisions didn't go his way he accepted them and moved forward. Throughout the trial he displayed an energy and affect that exuded self-confidence. He spoke loudly, clearly, and with animation. Despite the fact that at times he was equally as contentious as Darden, this isn't a description that would accurately characterize Cochran. He could be no surer of the final outcome than Darden, but up until the moment the verdict was announced, he looked and sounded like a winner.

These kinds of differences demonstrate the significant part that image and communication play in how we are perceived by others. The political arena provides yet another forum to examine this phenomenon. Perhaps the seminal defining moment of the importance of image was the Kennedy/Nixon debate of 1960. Although most of us can't remember the content of the debate, we do remember the physical appearance of the candidates as they sat on the platform. Despite the fact that Kennedy was in poor health, he looked youthful, tan, poised, and relaxed. Although only four years Kennedy's senior, Nixon (who refused to wear television makeup) looked wan and tired. In terms of outcome, polls of television viewers conducted after the debate gave Kennedy the edge, while polls of radio listeners reported Nixon the victor. From this point forward political candidates became constantly aware of the power of image to make or break their aspirations.

Dr. Allen Weiner, president of Communication Development Associates in Woodland Hills, California, has conducted research that suggests in day-to-day communication the impression that we make on others is based largely on how we look and sound. The following chart reveals that, in fact, a full 90 percent of that impression is based on factors related to other than what we actually say.

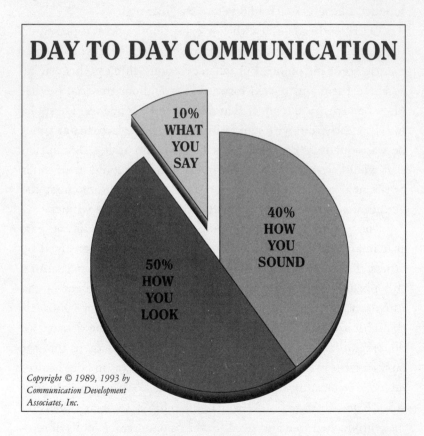

DAY TO DAY COMMUNICATION

10%
WHAT
YOU
SAY

40%
HOW
YOU
SOUND

50%
HOW
YOU
LOOK

Copyright © 1989, 1993 by
Communication Development
Associates, Inc.

Before reading further, check off the items below with which you agree. This list will help you to assess the degree to which you are aware of the importance of the image that you present and the manner in which you communicate.

_____ I know that image is important; therefore, I take special care to dress in a manner consistent with my position.

_____ I think before I speak, taking care to express my message succinctly and effectively.

_____ I pay special attention to grooming: hair, nails, skin, makeup (women), facial hair (men), hands, teeth, etc.

_____ My shoes are always shined.

_____ My body language suggests confidence and poise.

_____ I am no more than fifteen pounds over- or underweight.

_____ My clothes are always freshly pressed when I begin the day.

_____ I know what colors look best on me, and I use that to my advantage.

_____ I am practiced at making presentations in front of a group.

_____ I typically maintain my composure under pressure.

_____ My breath and body are free from unpleasant or offensive odors.

_____ I have no heavy regional accent that might detract from my message.

Image

A rule of thumb in business is that you should not dress for the job that you _have,_ but rather dress for the one that you _want._ Look around your organization and make a mental note of what people at the next level up from yours are wearing. If you are in a manufacturing environment, you may need to look several levels up. Here is where you'll find your greatest clues for how you should look when you go to work. As much as you may not like it, the fact is that your credibility is, in part, determined by the degree to which you look neat, crisp, professionally attired, and well groomed.

I can recall my mother preaching during my teens that I should always iron my clothes and look in the mirror twice before I went out. After all, she would warn, you never know who you are going to run into (and heaven forbid that I should be a bad reflection on my upbringing!). Arguments always ensued about what was more important—what's on the inside or the outside? Like many teenagers, I wanted my identity to be based on who I was, not what I was wearing. Many adults today continue to cling to that teenage opinion. They think that what's inside will supersede what's outside. All these years later I think that Mom was right. We *are* judged on our appearance first, and on who we are second—if we are fortunate enough to have a second chance. Many times we never have the opportunity for a second chance because we're written off before it comes.

The issue of dress has been the topic of many discussions, of late, particularly among women (men's workplace "uniforms" have remained relatively static). Whereas it was unusual as recently as five years ago to find women dressed in pants in most corporations, today it has become commonplace. When I remarked during a Leadership Skills for Women program (at which all of the participants were wearing pants) that wearing pants would not likely move them up the corporate ladder, I was met with overwhelming resistance from this group of thirty-something-aged women. Several protested that their pant outfits were just as expensive and stylish as the dresses worn by the more senior executive women. The cost of your apparel is not as important as the fact that those people in corporations who make hiring and promotion decisions *still* view dresses and skirt suits as more professional. If you are aiming at upward mobility, then you need to adopt a more conservative form of dress.

This same topic arose during a casual conversation with a friend who is the director of nursing at a hospital in the Los Angeles area. I commented that the professionalism of nursing seemed to have declined since staff members were no longer required to wear uniforms. Her response, and one with which I agree, is that it is tough to get this generation of employees to conform and that she would rather have a qualified and competent employee than one simply in a white uniform. But the answer isn't that simple. We are always affected by others' perceptions of us. If I had a dollar for each time I told a client, "Perception is reality," I'd be a rich woman.

People will always make assumptions about our competence based on how we look. When a nurse wearing a pair of jeans and a wrinkled blouse appears at my bedside, I somehow believe that she is less competent than someone wearing a starched white uniform. Is this true? Is one really more competent than the other? Of course not. Your image only gets you in the door. As with all of the coaching hints contained in this book, being concerned about your image is meaningless unless you back it up with the goods—capable performance. It makes a lot more sense, however, to start the interaction, whether it be between a nurse and a patient, an interviewer and a candidate, or a sales clerk and a customer, with a leg up. Remember, *you sell the sizzle, not the steak.*

Maybe a real-time example will help here. George was an accounting manager in a small division of a major apparel manufacturer. He grew up in a Pennsylvania coal mining town. He was a son of working-class parents, and the oldest of eight children. His father was the union steward of his mine. Always small for his age, George grew up knowing how to take care of himself with both his fists and his tongue. He could be described as *scrappy*. He put himself through college at night while working days in a coal mine and, at the same time, raising his own family.

George used to go to work casually dressed in slacks and a short-sleeved shirt—certainly a step up from his mining days. His favorite shoes were a pair of worn, black, soft-sole loafers—the kind that you can't polish (which he obviously didn't care to try). His gray hair was wiry and often unkempt. The guy was brilliant. He was, without a doubt, the most technically competent manager in his division, but a bit of a rebel. He didn't seem to care how others dressed, he didn't need to be like them, and he didn't care about what they thought of him. He knew that he *knew his stuff*.

When the brass from corporate visited the plant, however, they often ignored George's remarks at meetings and overlooked his valuable suggestions for how to improve bottom-line profits. No matter what he said or how he said it, he couldn't get them to take him seriously. He became increasingly frustrated, belligerent, and intolerant of others. He knew what he was saying made sense, but he couldn't get anyone to listen to him.

One day, after a trip to the corporate offices, George appeared at the office in a navy blue suit, red power tie, well-shined black leather shoes, and with hair neatly styled. He looked ten years younger and every bit the executive that he was. It was interesting to watch his staff interact with him. Although George had not fundamentally changed who he was, others treated him with more respect and deference. After a while, George actually started to act differently. Always a bit brash and too quick to speak in the past, he now weighed his words carefully and took care not to step on too many toes. He gave new meaning to the adage *clothes make the man*. Within two years, George had been promoted out of his small division and into the corporate accounting office. Within five years, he was named vice president of one of the company's up-and-coming divisions.

George is a terrific example of someone who overcame his strengths: technical expertise and staunch independence. No one knows who or what persuaded George to change his dress, and ultimately his behavior, but it prevented George from derailing from an otherwise successful career. Just as coworkers judged George, people judge us every day by how we look. Before we even open our mouths, people have made a mental judgment about us based on how we are dressed, how we carry ourselves, and the demeanor with which we present ourselves. Within thirty seconds, a first impression is formed, so you had better make that the best impression possible—it can make the difference in someone giving you the edge or simply dismissing you.

If you think this isn't right, or that's not how you judge others, think again. We are all guilty of doing the same thing. How many times have you walked up to a particularly well-dressed person in a department store and asked for help, only to be told that he or she didn't work there? Or, have you made an assumption about someone's intelligence based on his or her appearance? Which one of us would look at scientist and author Stephen Hawking, who is wheelchair bound because of his disabilities, and think that he is one of the most brilliant individuals on the face of the earth? This is the same difficult phenomenon that so many people with visible disabilities encounter. Hawking's phenomenal intellectual ability, however, is enough to eclipse his looks. Most of us don't possess such extraordinary talent, and assumptions are made based on very little information. This is why it's so important to leverage image so that the first impression is at worst a neutral one and at best a positive one.

When Less Is More

Is it possible to pay too much attention to your looks and look too good? YES! On a continuum from one to ten, with one being slovenly and ten being glamorous, your appearance should probably be around a seven or eight. Going to work is not going out on a date. Women tend to have more difficulty with this particular problem than men, although I've seen extraordinarily handsome men encounter similar problems.

It is a fine line between well dressed and provocative. Cologne or perfume should be kept to a minimum. Jewelry is meant to complement an outfit. Even though Madison Avenue may dictate pants, short skirt lengths, or garish fashions, it's better to be safe than sorry in most businesses (the fashion and entertainment industries may be the exceptions). Take a moderate approach. One woman executive says that after she's finished dressing in the morning, she stands with her back to the mirror then quickly swings around. If any one thing stands out, she removes it.

Both men and women who are blessed with outstanding looks encounter much the same difficulties. Both men and women can be thought of as *dumb blonds*. One businessman whom I coached, Jeff, could be described as drop-dead gorgeous. He had a George Hamilton tan, was blond, trim, and impeccably groomed. He could easily pass for a model. During the course of our coaching, Jeff revealed that as a teenager he was the classic ninety-pound weakling. Years of working out and special attention to his looks had transformed this fellow into an Adonis. He admitted that he was obsessed with his looks and never left the house without being the picture of perfection.

Jeff's good looks, combined with native intelligence, landed him in his career as a sales representative for a pharmaceutical firm. His problem was that people didn't take him seriously. They couldn't get past his looks. His colleagues tended to feel somewhat inferior in his presence and sabotaged his efforts by withholding essential information and upstaging him at sales conferences. His defense mechanism for overcoming childhood trauma was getting in his way. The coaching focused extensively on getting Jeff to grow into his adult role and not act out of childhood pain. At the same time, I gave him several suggestions for downplaying his looks in ways that would immediately change how others perceived him: trade in his colored contacts for a pair of glasses; wear plain, inexpensive ties instead of bold ones that called attention; let his hair grow slightly longer and out of its precision cut; and exchange manicures for doing his nails himself.

It wasn't easy for him, but Jeff's desire to avoid derailment gave him the courage to look different. A secondary gain for Jeff from the change in physical appearance was that he no longer needed to be a perfectionist in other ways. He tended to be less cautious in his choice of words and acted more like one of the guys. Within several months, Jeff found people responding to his messages rather than to him as the messenger, and his relationships with his peers began to improve. More important, Jeff felt better about himself.

Like many people who are coached, Jeff was fearful that he would lose his entire identity if he did anything different. In reality, however, coaching, or self-coaching, is about moving from out of bounds to back onto the playing field. It is not about terminating behavior, but rather about turning down the volume on those behaviors that are putting you out of bounds. It is about building complementary skills or behaviors.

What Does Your Body Say About You?

Another aspect of image is body language. Awareness of how you present yourself is critical to avoiding derailment. The three most important areas of which you should be aware are face, hands, and posture. Combined, these can shout that you are fearful and insecure or that you are comfortable and confident.

I once watched an interview with retired U.S. Army General Colin Powell and was struck by how comfortable he seemed with himself, the interviewer, and the world in general. I analyzed what gave me this impression, and it came down to how he looked and sounded (the latter I'll save for a bit later in this chapter). I realized that it boiled down to his face, hands, and posture. When seated, Powell had his hands loosely interlocked in his lap, moved them when he gestured, then unobtrusively returned them to the original position. Throughout the interview, I watched him do this countless times. It gave the impression of comfortable professionalism. Contrast this with someone who fidgets with a pen, tightly clings to the sides of a chair, or drums his or her fingers. The message somehow just isn't the same.

Then I watched as Powell listened to the interviewer's questions. His eyes stayed on the reporter, his head nodded with understanding and he sat upright, but not rigidly, in his chair. With the toughest of questions Powell remained the same, never shifting in discomfort or wincing at the deep probes. He smiled when it was appropriate and didn't when he wanted to convey that his message was serious. I turned to someone in the room who is less attuned than I am to matters pertaining to image and communication and commented that Powell seemed so comfortable with himself. The response, "I was just thinking the same thing," speaks to the fact that others do notice these things about us. Whether he was trained to do so or it comes naturally to him, Powell provides a model of confidence and ease with himself and others.

Smiling presents a unique problem for women and people of certain cultures. In another workshop on leadership skills for women, a petite woman engineer working for a major airline proclaimed that no one ever took her seriously, and she said it with a big smile on her face. Everyone in the room laughed because they could immediately see the problem. Smiles should be used to communicate happiness, levity, or joking, not serious messages. The smile totally diminished the serious nature of the woman's message. Unfortunately, women frequently use smiling as a means of softening their messages to avoid appearing too strong. Most women could smile less, choose the times when they smile more carefully, and avoid using a smile to ward off criticism.

Paradoxically, smiling can be used as a valuable tool for both men and women in their repertoires of skills—provided the feedback that you get from others is that you're too serious, staid, or intimidating. This was the case with a man I coached not long ago. The intensity with which he delivered his messages frequently overwhelmed his colleagues. He was tall, assertive, smart, and always on target, but people were intimidated by him and wouldn't respond when he asked for their opinions of his ideas. I knew that he recently became a father and asked how he talked to his child. With this, a big smile came to his face with a softness that warmed my heart. When I suggested that he think about the child when speaking with his colleagues he looked at me incredulously. Certainly I couldn't be serious. He thought that people would perceive him as being too soft. In fact, his other characteristics would overshadow this slight change in facial expression. This was another example of adding to the repertoire rather than taking something away. With this change, and some other coaching hints that he practiced, people began to describe him as more approachable and easier to talk to.

Posture is yet another means by which we reveal our self-esteem. How many times have you seen someone in a meeting slouched down in a chair or hunched over the table leaning on one elbow? Or, have you ever noted a statuesque woman who walks a bit hunched over so as not to appear too tall? Although rigidity is not the order of the day, good posture conveys the message that *I am someone to contend with*. Your posture increases the perception of credibility and confidence before you ever open your mouth. Look at U.S. Attorney General Janet Reno. Her posture and other body language play no small part in our perception of her credibility. I recently found myself in the same elevator with Reno and was struck by her powerful presence. Despite being blamed for the incidents at Waco and Ruby Ridge, Reno has thus far managed to avoid derailment largely because of her image and communication style.

One last suggestion about how you look. This one comes from communication specialist Dr. Allen Weiner, who was mentioned earlier in this chapter. When people stand in front of a room making a presentation or being introduced, they often appear uncomfortable, largely because they don't know what to do with their hands. They will put them in their pockets, fold them in front of them (Weiner calls this the fig leaf approach), or clasp them behind their backs—all the while looking none too comfortable. Weiner suggests that hands be kept with fingers loosely clasped at about the same height you would hold a glass while standing at a cocktail party. Similarly, when gesturing in front of groups, hands should be kept at about the same height and moved no wider apart than as if you were holding a basketball. The exception being when speaking before large groups where more pronounced gestures are required and would not likely detract from the message.

Communication

Let's revisit another set of debates. The first is the television debate that took place during the 1988 presidential campaign when Dan Quayle ran for vice president as George Bush's running mate. At one point, he found himself debating his challenger, Lloyd Bentsen. In contrast to the stately and comfortable Bentsen, Quayle appeared anxious, his speaking voice was hesitant, his messages were incoherent, and his body language lacked confidence. With the sound turned off on the television, Quayle paled next to his elder colleague. With the sound on it was even worse. He looked and sounded nothing like the seasoned, statesmanlike vice presidents to whom we'd become accustomed. Regardless of your political persuasion, you must admit that Lyndon Johnson, Hubert Humphrey, Nelson Rockefeller, and George Bush all presented themselves confidently and credibly.

Four years later, Quayle was on the podium debating Al Gore and Ross Perot's running mate, Captain James B. Stockdale. After just a few minutes, I thought to myself, "This guy's been coached!" His positions on the issues were clearly stated, he used emphatic gestures to punctuate his remarks, and his body language was relaxed and controlled. Perhaps, in his role as vice president, he simply had become more comfortable in front of the cameras, but throughout his tenure he had been prone to such malapropisms and misstatements that it's doubtful that experience alone could be the reason for the transformation.

Dan Quayle provides us with a particularly poignant example of how early coaching can help to prevent derailment. Quayle was coached too late. Had he been coached early in the 1988 campaign, perhaps his term in office would have been significantly different and both he *and* Bush would have won in 1992. When it comes to communication, it is important to remember that we live in a sound-bite society. We measure people's abilities and judge their effectiveness in brief bits and pieces that we absorb during a moment in time. Once we *look* the part, the next important step is to *sound* the part.

Communication is made up of a number of components: accent or dialect, thought patterns as expressed in speech, and the actual sound of the speech itself. Each contributes to the overall impression of knowledge and credibility. Remember the pie chart at the beginning of this chapter: 50 percent of the impressions others have of you is based on how you look and 40 percent on how you sound. Only 10 percent is based on what you actually say. The importance of how you sound is embodied in a Chinese saying: "May you have a wonderful idea and not be able to convince anyone of it."

The Sexes' Differences in Communication

Before going further, I should mention that there are well-defined differences between how men and women communicate. My own experience indicates that many women tend to use words and sentence structures that are less direct than those of their male counterparts and, therefore, these women are less likely to be heard or taken seriously.

For example, I was playing tennis one morning and my ball went into the next court. I waited until the two men playing had finished their point, then said, "I think that's my ball behind you." Now, I didn't just *think* it was my ball, I knew *full well* that it was my ball because I watched it roll to a stop. Instead of just tossing it back, one of the men asked, "What are you playing with?" (referring to the brand of ball). He looked at the ball and then asked, "What number?" I realized that had I simply called over "Thank you," and nodded toward my ball, which is the custom on tennis courts, the entire scenario would have been different. By adding the words *I think* to my message I conveyed uncertainty, when in fact I wasn't the least bit uncertain. In essence, I caused him to doubt my credibility.

The tennis courts may be an odd place to identify differences in the sexes' communication, but the differences occur in boardrooms as well and make a significant difference in whose ideas are ultimately acknowledged and utilized. Here are five fatal errors that I've noticed that women make more frequently than men when they communicate.

1. **ASKING PERMISSION.** Although this may appear on the surface to be fairly benign, it in fact puts the woman in a subservient position. In our society, we expect children to ask permission, not adults. When women ask permission, they set themselves up to hear "no."

EXAMPLE: *Would it be all right if I took next Wednesday off for my son's graduation?*

In the same situation a man would say:

Just thought I'd let you know, I'll be out next Wednesday.

He assumes that if there is a problem with this his boss will tell him. This very situation arose during a team building that I did in the Midwest several years ago. The women complained that they were expected to ask permission to exceed their monthly budgets, but their male colleagues just informed the boss of such an occurrence. To the boss's credit, he admitted that he did subconsciously expect women to ask permission and changed his expectations.

2. **USING PREAMBLES.** Words soften a message, not strengthen it. The longer you talk, the more you dilute an effective message and lose the attention of the listener. Women soften their messages by using more words when fewer will do.

> **EXAMPLE:** *Would this be a good time to talk to you about something? Thanks. Well, I've been going over our accounts payable system. Did you know that this system was devised over fifteen years ago? That's an awfully long time to be using the same system. A friend of mine over at XYZ Company tells me that in the same time span they've revised their system four or five times. Ours is really antiquated. Well, maybe not antiquated, but certainly in need of looking at. Anyway, where was I? Oh, yeah, improving the accounts payable system. It would appear to me that one of the problems lies in how payables are logged when they arrive. We get so many dunning notices and even wind up paying a lot in late fees because of it. Last month alone we must have paid nearly 5 percent of the total payables in late fees. I'm not really sure why this happens, since we've got plenty of people in the department working on it. . . .*

At this point the boss wants to scream, "What's your point?"—and rightly so. Far too many words were used before ever getting to the main point, and more important, the causes of and solutions to the problem. Managers want their staff members to *solve* problems, not create more. This woman suffers from a serious case of the *preambles*. How could she strengthen her message? Perhaps like this:

*I need about five minutes of your time to discuss something impor-
tant. There's clearly a problem in our accounts payable system.
Bills are long overdue, and we're unnecessarily paying excessive
late fees. I just wanted you to know that I'm working on a system to revise the current process, so if you have any ideas for short-
ening the payment cycle based on your experience you might want
to join our brainstorming session next Friday.*

Crisp. Clear. To the point. Within thirty seconds the boss knows
what the problem is, that it's going to be fixed, and that he or she
is invited to be part of the process of solving the problem.

3. **ASKING QUESTIONS INSTEAD OF MAKING STATE-
MENTS.** This technique was invented by our foremothers as a
means of getting their two cents in without appearing too aggressive. In business, however, a woman leaves herself open to a cri-
tique of the idea, rather than a discussion of the value of it, when
she couches her opinions in the form of questions.

EXAMPLE: *What would you think about moving toward a
smorgasbord approach to employee benefits?*

The savvy listener knows that this really is not a question. The
speaker has an idea that she is trying to further, but by putting it
as a question she obscures that fact. In contrast, this approach
would be much more effective:

*It seems to me it's time to move in a new direction with regard to
employee benefits. I think the smorgasbord approach merits examination for the following reasons. . . .*

The second example states the case, provides backup data, and expects a discussion based on merit rather than on the whim or
goodwill of the boss.

4. **APOLOGIZING.** Women apologize significantly more frequently than men, *even when no apology is necessary*. A woman's self-image is increasingly eroded with each apology.

> **EXAMPLE:** *A boss gives his female assistant a large graphics project with very clear directions. She follows those directions to a T and presents him with the results* before *the deadline. He looks at the project and says it's not how he wants it. He then proceeds to change the instructions and asks that it be redone. Nine times out of ten, the woman will say,* "I'm sorry, I didn't realize that's what you wanted. I'll redo it."

Don't get me wrong. There's a time and place for apologies. That time and place, however, is when a large, costly, or high-profile mistake is made. Even then, men are hard-pressed to get the apology through their lips. Women's apologies are frequently inappropriate and demean them. My most frequent coaching suggestion for women is *stop apologizing.*

5. **EXPLAINING AD NAUSEAM.** This is at the other end of the preamble. A woman has now asked permission, couched her opinion in the form of a question, used a lot of words to get to her point, perhaps apologized in the process—*and now she explains some more!* Now, I must admit that this is not always her fault. Especially when she's communicating with a man. Many times men will fail to use body language, such as head nods or verbal remarks, that indicate that they have heard what's been said. Therefore, the woman talks more, thinking that she hasn't been understood. She explains her point two or three times, waiting for some acknowledgment of the message. Women, take care to say it once. Let silence be a powerful tool in prodding the other person into responding; you are not responsible for the entire communication.

With very subtle modifications, women can change the manner in which they are perceived. Here are eight things that *both* men and women can do to put more power behind their messages:

1. **MAKE CERTAIN YOUR HANDSHAKE IS FIRM.** The handshake can be the very first thing you use to convey the message "I'm someone to be contended with." Women have asked me if it's appropriate for them to extend their hand first. Absolutely! Being the first to extend your hand in greeting, combined with a firm handshake, communicates control and confidence. Use them to your advantage.

2. **DRESS APPROPRIATELY.** "Dress for the job you want, not the job you have" remains your best guide for being taken seriously.

3. **USE "I" STATEMENTS.** Don't be afraid to begin your sentences with "I." What many of us learned in grade school about never starting a sentence with "I" (because it sounds too egotistical) doesn't hold true in business. If you are giving your own opinion, then own it with statements like "I believe," "I contend," "I would expect," or "I feel strongly."

4. **MAKE DIRECT EYE CONTACT.** Although you don't want to stare someone down and make them uncomfortable by never averting your eyes from theirs, looking someone directly in the eye when you are giving your opinion does add a certain amount of credibility to your message. When someone is able to look us in the eye, we believe he or she is speaking the truth.

5. **KNOW YOUR SUBJECT.** You've already heard it several times in this book: "Nothing takes the place of technical competence." When you know your subject, you speak with a certainty that is impossible to convey when you're unsure. You can build a base of technical knowledge that adds to your confidence by getting a college degree, taking classes or workshops, reading technical journals, or networking with other professionals in your field.

6. **PEPPER YOUR CONVERSATION WITH THE OTHER PERSON'S NAME.** When you want to get children to listen to you,

you use their names when speaking to them. A similar tactic works equally well in business conversations. You don't want to sound like a used car salesperson, but you do want to keep the other person's attention.

7. **MAKE AFFIRMATIVE STATEMENTS.** Instead of couching your comments in the form of questions, turn them into affirmative statements, beginning with an "I" message. Change "What would you think if we" to "I think that we should." The latter conveys much more certainty and influence.

8. **GET TO THE POINT.** Dr. Allen Weiner developed a technique that he calls "bottom-line communication." His research indicates that when you make your main point the first thing that comes out of your mouth, and support it with several key facts, you are more likely to avoid using preambles and explaining ad nauseam. Don't obscure the most important part of your message with a lot of words; give it clearly up front.

Georgetown University Professor Deborah Tannen is the author of several wonderful books and articles on the subject of sex differences in communication. A number of her theories confirm my observation of the five fatal errors discussed earlier. The September–October 1995 issue of *Harvard Business Review* contains her outstanding article "The Power of Talk: Who Gets Heard and Why," in which she asserts, "Women are likely to downplay their certainty; men are likely to minimize their doubts." I recommend reading the article or her book about workplace communication, *Talking from 9 to 5*. It helps both men and women understand ways in which they may be more effective in communicating with members of the opposite sex.

Accents and Dialects

The issue of accents and dialects is a sensitive one that needs to be considered in light of our rich heritage as a melting pot, welcoming of people from all nations and backgrounds. Although some may find it offensive, or inappropriate for discussion here, the words of my friend and colleague Susan Picascia ring in my ear: *A good coach has the courage to speak the unspoken.* Therefore, I would find it an unconscionable error of omission to avoid a discussion about accents and dialects.

As the complexion of society changes, both literally and figuratively, so do our impressions about expecting others to look and sound the same in the microcosm called work. If the stereotypes of fifty years ago prevailed, the workforce would still be predominantly white and male. Similarly, if we continue to perpetuate the stereotype of how people should sound in the workplace, everyone would be accentless—sounding somewhat like newscasters who are hired partly for their ability to speak without an accent. The goal of this discussion is not to encourage homogeneity, but rather to illuminate the ways in which strong accents and dialects can be potential career derailers.

As a Jewish woman, I am all too aware of the fact that what appear to be legitimate workplace expectations can be guises for prejudice and discrimination. Likewise, I know that I must constantly be vigilant about crossing the line between expression of my individuality and being heard and seen in the most favorable light possible so that I can achieve my goals. Just as I wouldn't wear blue jeans to a meeting with a new client, in that same meeting I wouldn't use the Yiddish jargon that I learned growing up. On the other hand, even if it might in some way damage my career, I wouldn't hesitate to decline an invitation to a private club from which women or people of color are excluded. The goal is to increase the likelihood of success by playing the corporate game within commonly accepted bounds, *without compromising your principles or ethical standards.*

There are numerous examples of successful people who have strong accents. As the United States continues to establish multinational firms, those numbers will increase and bring with them greater tolerance for other than "newscaster" accents. I simply ask you to consider how your accent or dialect might be perceived by others. Can you be clearly understood? Do you use phrases or jargon that, while acceptable in your neighborhood, are not commonly used by your workplace peers? Does your accent diminish your self-confidence when speaking before groups or at meetings? Do you feel as if your vocabulary is not sufficient for fluid conversation?

If you answer yes to any of these questions, or if you believe that your manner of speaking has impeded your progress, then you may want to consider doing something about it. Accent-reduction schools and elocution classes are available in most major cities. Conversely, if you believe it is too great a compromise to refrain from using certain jargon or to reduce your accent, *don't do it*. Like all of the other suggestions contained in this book, it is one more factor to consider in your effort to avoid derailment.

Sam was on the verge of derailment but didn't have a clue why. Neither did his boss. She asked me to coach him, saying his career was stalled despite the fact that he was a good, solid performer. Higher-ups in the European shipping company where he worked began asking that Sam be excluded from certain meetings, particularly those at which clients were present. No matter how hard she tried to find out what the problem was, people were never forthcoming with an answer.

My first meeting with Sam took place in his office in Miami Beach. When his secretary ushered me in, Sam stood and extended his hand to greet me. He was well dressed, neatly groomed, and had an engaging smile. So far so good. When he began to speak, however, the problem became readily apparent, because Sam spoke with a thick Cuban accent. He also spoke quickly and in long rambling sentences so that it was difficult to understand him and follow his train of thought. Several times during the conversation, I had to ask him to slow down.

We then proceeded to a nearby upscale restaurant for lunch. People appeared to know Sam and greeted him with friendly waves. Another point in his favor, I noted. He is a relationship builder. Over lunch I listened to Sam talk about his career, how he got to where he was, what he thought might be the problem, and how he was now working harder than ever in hopes of turning the situation around. I also observed his behavior as he ate his meal. Strike two. He began by tucking the linen napkin into his collar, then breaking and buttering a roll before the bread plates were on the table, making an awful mess in the process. During the meal, he talked with his mouth full of food, unaware of how it might appear to others.

Over the course of several coaching sessions I learned more about Sam. He was from a poor family who emigrated from Cuba in the 1950s. His parents believed in education and worked hard to make certain that their son could go to college. He was the superstar of the family, the only one to have a blossoming career. In turn, he worked long, hard hours to get where he was and to feel worthy of the efforts his parents had made on his behalf. He truly believed that working harder, turning up the volume on what he did best, was the answer to his problems.

Between sessions I spoke with Sam's boss to determine whether my assessment that productivity was not the problem was in fact true. She confirmed my hunch that he was always willing to go the extra mile and produced what was expected of him and more. Why, I wondered, was no one willing to tell him that his accent, rambling monologues, and table manners were about to derail him? Speaking with his boss a bit longer, I found out that Sam had worked for her at her previous job as well. In total, they had worked together for more than twenty years. She was so accustomed to him and his habits that she never noticed that he had reached a stage in his career where they were no longer acceptable. She was too close to the situation. As for the higher-ups, they probably were too embarrassed, or fearful of being called snobby, to help Sam to get back in bounds.

It is one of the tougher jobs of a coach to talk about behaviors as personal as accents and table manners. It's a lot easier to suggest letting your hair grow longer. Nevertheless, Sam was coached in these areas and he responded immediately. He enrolled in an accent-reduction class, followed my instructions for table manners, and took care to speak in shorter, better-defined sentences. Unfortunately, his senior management wouldn't give him a chance and directed his boss to fire Sam, which she did with great personal anguish. The coaching was not wasted, however. As often happens when individuals are *freed up to find new opportunities* (fired), they go on to find a position better suited for them. Such is the case with Sam. He is now back on his career track in another organization that highly values his abilities and appreciates his efforts. Without the coaching, he might have found himself in the same situation over and over again until he overcame his strengths.

Thought Patterns

As I mentioned in Sam's case, the ability to speak cogently and concisely contributes to others' perception of us. Except in unusual circumstances when the speaker or material being conveyed is extraordinarily compelling, people can listen to only relatively brief, clearly ordered messages and actually comprehend them. Countless messages are lost entirely when the speaker rambles on long after his or her point has been made. In videotaping workplace interactions, I'm struck by the number of times a speaker makes a point, then explains it, makes the point again, and explains it once more. As the camera pans the room, it reveals undeniably bored, uninterested faces straining to listen politely until the speaker has finished.

The person who rambles also loses his or her audience. Returning to Colin Powell for a moment, it was clear from the interview I saw that his credibility is in part due to his speech patterns. Each time he was asked a question he directly answered the question using clear, succinct sentences. If he didn't have an answer, he said so. There was no fat to be trimmed and no misunderstanding about where he stood.

Here is an example of how disorganized thought patterns ineffectively convey the message, lose the listener's interest, and diminish the speaker's credibility in the process:

Boss: *Do you think we should change our marketing strategy next year?*
Employee: *Well, that's a good question. I guess there are a number of different ways of looking at it. If we were to continue along the same path we're on, that is if we were to not make any changes that might upset the applecart, it's possible, maybe we might—that is, some people think that we're going along the right path now and with a few minor variations could, well, there's a chance that the numbers might increase a bit over last year's sales, but I'm not really sure myself. It seems to me that we've changed the strategy a number of times in the past year or two, well actually maybe five years, and in most cases, with a few exceptions, the results were average, so you could say they were effective, but nothing really spectacular happened. On the other hand, take a look at what our competitors have done for the past few years and looks like they're marginally edging us out. Of course, there's ABC Company, which did a lot worse than we did, but that's only because they sold off one of their cash cows. So, I guess it might be worth a try to . . .*

Even writing this script was painful, let alone listening to it! Yet it's not so far from how people answer questions every day in corporate America. The major mistakes made by the speaker include:

- failure to express a point of view
- soft word choices (e.g., maybe, I guess, we might)

- rambling thought process
- incomplete sentences and ideas
- too much playing "devil's advocate"

Let's replay the same scenario, this time using a more Powellesque approach:

Boss: *Do you think we should change our marketing strategy next year?*

Employee: [Pause to think] *Definitely not. Our current strategy has only been in place for less than a year and is already yielding very promising results. There's been a 10 percent increase in sales despite a sluggish market, which forecasts well for next year when the market is expected to pick up.*

Who seems more credible to you? The first or second employee? In fewer than fifty words, the second employee clearly communicated his or her opinion as well as provided a rationale for it. Sam was coached to do the same thing with four *pretty darn simple steps:*

1. (Pretty)   Pause a moment to collect your thoughts. Don't answer immediately.
2. (Darn)   Directly answer the question that was asked.
3. (Simple)   Support your answer with facts or knowledge.
4. (Steps)   Stop.

Getting and Keeping Audience Attention

According to Shakespeare, all the world's a stage, and we humans are merely players. The workplace can be considered just another set and scene. For most people, however, the anticipation of making a presentation, be it to a group of five people or fifty, engenders a sense of fear second only to that of dying on the list of things

Americans fear most. Yet we present ourselves and our ideas all the time. The next time you have to give a public speech, think of it as actors do—as an *opportunity* to create a special way of sending a message and make a lasting, and positive, impression.

The following are a few simple coaching hints, recommended by Dr. Douglas Andrews, a University of Southern California professor and communications coach, to help you become an influential player on the corporate stage.

1. **NEVER GIVE A PRESENTATION YOU HAVEN'T PREPARED.** The saying *chance favors the prepared mind* is never more true than when speaking before an audience. Unless you are one of the few gifted people who can speak extemporaneously in front of groups, you can't afford to wait until the day of your presentation to prepare. Even if you only jot down a few notes on index cards, you're more likely to remember the key points and avoid aimless rambling. When planning on speaking to a few people, mentally rehearse what you plan to say, picture people listening attentively to you, and know when to stop.

2. **PRACTICE TO MUSIC.** If you tend to make a monotone, slow-paced presentation, begin practicing to a tune with an upbeat tempo. Don't use a Sousa march, but choose something that will help you keep a quick pace. Try using a metronome to overcome either slow and plodding presentations or the inclination to speak too fast. Keep in mind that when you speak too fast it can be a sign of lack of confidence. It gives the impression that you don't want to take up too much of the listener's time. Tempo is an important determinant of the impression one has of your message.

3. **BREAK UP YOUR PRESENTATION.** Another way of avoiding long monologues is to break up your presentation into smaller pieces and focus on changing one aspect of each piece when it's delivered. For example, make a notation to slow down during one particular piece, to speak more quickly during the next, and to use

hand gestures during the next. Alternate these behaviors through-out the presentation until they look and sound natural. Underline words that you want to emphasize and indicate when you want to look directly at the faces in the crowd.

4. **USE PACE TO ALTER PITCH.** If your voice unnaturally goes up several octaves the moment you speak in front of a room full of people, or when the spotlight shifts to you during a meeting, try speaking a bit more slowly. As you slow down your speech, your voice tends to drop as well.

5. **USE SHORT WORDS.** Giving a presentation is not the time to impress others with your command of the English language by using long, obscure words. Not only is your audience likely to think it pretentious, you're more likely to forget or mispronounce them. Don't feel compelled to use a dollar word when a quarter one will do. It's easier for the listeners to process the message, it doesn't challenge them, and you tend to enunciate shorter words clearly.

6. **USE BODY ENGLISH.** Don't forget the importance of body language. Good posture, direct eye contact, and subtle gestures combine to give the impression of confidence and credibility.

7. **USE A CAMCORDER.** Here's a place to make good use of the family video camera. Videotape yourself practicing a presentation. Critically assess what you can do to be more effective, and don't be afraid to ask the family for feedback. Sometimes they'll give you better coaching hints than anyone else!

Like it or not, the image that we portray and the communication style that we use are the first two things that others notice about us—and they contribute significantly to the impression that we make. Fortunately, they are also two of the more simple factors to address when considering how to avoid premature derailment. Think of them as tools that you can use to your advantage. Develop your own unique style, but fine-tune that style so that it works *for* you rather than *against* you.

Strategies for Improving Image

1. Get a good barber or hairdresser.
2. Don't scrimp when it comes to spending money on work clothes.
3. Never leave the house before looking in the mirror twice.
4. Manicure your nails once a week.
5. Check the shine, heels, and soles of your shoes, especially before an important meeting.
6. Use smiles, head nods, and other facial expressions to soften messages.
7. Use appropriate pacing and gestures to strengthen messages.
8. Read *Letitia Baldrige's New Complete Guide to Executive Manners* (see page 247).
9. If there's something about your appearance that you're so self-conscious of that it affects your self-confidence, have it colored, cut, plugged, removed, lifted, tucked, or otherwise surgically altered!
10. If your corrected vision leaves you with Coke bottles, switch to contact lenses or high-index glasses.
11. Exercise regularly—it improves your physical health, self-image, and outlook.
12. Absent intervening medical factors, try to stay within ten to fifteen pounds of your ideal body weight.
13. Dress for the job you want, not the job you have.
14. Wear knee-length socks or other appropriate hosiery.

S trategies for Improving Communication

15. Join Toastmaster's International (see page 241) to gain composure and confidence when speaking before groups.

16. Take an acting class to increase fluidity of expression.

17. Use a firm, "I'm someone to be contended with" handshake.

18. Think about what you want to say before you say it.

19. Consider an accent-reduction or elocution class.

20. Practice important presentations in advance.

21. Use mental imagery to "see" what you're going to say and picture a positive response from the audience.

22. When using notes during a presentation, use index cards instead of sheets of paper (the cards will be less conspicuous in the event that your hands begin to shake).

23. Use simple, easy-to-understand words.

24. Use the four Pretty Darn Simple Steps to mentally prepare your responses.

Insensitivity to the Reactions of Others

CRAFT A WINNING PERSONALITY

The CEO of an internationally known manufacturing firm recently mentioned in passing that his highly competent, well-educated staff would soon need coaching and training on how to be less "technocratic." Because the company is a leader in its field and has always prided itself on choosing the cream of the crop from the most prestigious business schools, this came as somewhat of a surprise. When I probed into the CEO's sudden change of heart, he explained that his customers had begun complaining about the condescending and arrogant attitudes that his staff brought to their interactions. In fact, they were in jeopardy of losing their biggest client because of it. In spite of this senior management team's technical competence, the customer doesn't want to work with them.

If you are eccentric (but smart), difficult (but gifted), or an oddball (but a whiz), you're destined to derail. You can't stay competitive if you do not have a winning personality. This chapter is about the behaviors that comprise a winning personality. Difficult to measure and describe, personality is noticed and judged in nearly every interaction. A pleasing personality includes having self-confidence and insight into how you affect others, relating to all kinds of people and making them feel easy around you, knowing that you don't have to control everyone and everything, striving to act with integrity at all times, treating others the way you would want to be treated, and acting graciously even in the most difficult situations.

The following checklist should help you assess your own personality.

_____ I am aware of how others perceive me.

_____ I keep my personal moods out of the office.

_____ Others would describe me as even-tempered.

_____ It's more important to me that the project gets completed than for me to get credit for its completion.

_____ I generally tell people where I stand on various issues so that they're not left guessing.

_____ People have told me that they enjoy working with me.

_____ I am generally aware of other people's moods.

_____ I can laugh at my mistakes when the situation calls for it.

_____ I know the difference between being assertive and being aggressive and typically opt for the former.

_____ It's hard to recall a time when I've embarrassed someone by one of my remarks.

_____ I look waiters and waitresses in the eye when I speak to them.

_____ I give others feedback as objectively as possible and always in private.

When you think about successful people with winning personalities, Lee Iacocca, Gloria Steinem, Magic Johnson, and Eleanor Roosevelt come to mind. Although it is difficult to know how public figures act in private, these examples appear to share the common traits of a strong sense of self, commitment to a cause greater than themselves, and a fundamental respect for all those whom they encounter on life's path. It is what makes up what is frequently called *character.* Legendary basketball coach John Wooden once said, "Be more concerned with your character than with your reputation. Your character is what you really are, while your reputation is merely what others think you are."

Conversely, when you think about successful people with personalities that are offensive, Newt Gingrich, Leona Helmsley, and Ross Perot come to mind. Their own needs precede their deeds and the needs of others. They may espouse a philosophy of benevolence, but it fails to ring true and is contradicted by their actions. I once observed tennis legend Martina Navratilova at a fund-raiser. As you might imagine, people were thrilled with the opportunity to meet her and many approached her to ask for an autograph. My high regard for her diminished with one act. When she obviously became tired of signing, she rolled her eyes and gave a disgusted look to one of her admirers who dared to ask for an autograph. The person walked away looking hurt and embarrassed. It was a reminder that it takes a lifetime to build a positive image, but only a moment to have it tarnished in the eyes of others.

The question that most frequently arises in discussions about character is, *Can character be developed or is it something that you're born with?* My own position is that not only *can* character be developed, but most people *do* develop it and are not born with it. It is unlikely that Gloria Steinem or Lee Iacocca was born with character. If anything, quite the opposite. Steinem was born to an emotionally unstable mother and, from an early age, was responsible for raising herself. Iacocca, the son of Italian immigrants, regularly faced the humiliation of classmates who taunted him for his ethnic upbringing. Although it could be argued that Steinem and Iacocca were *born* with the ability to overcome adversity, it is just as likely that they *learned* how to do so. Steinem and Iacocca are two reasons why I believe that a winning personality can be developed. Another reason is that I've seen people develop it—people like Joe.

To Change or Not to Change—That Is the Question

When Joe's boss told him that he had to go for coaching if he had any hope of keeping his job, Joe specifically requested that I be his coach. I had met Joe when we'd both served on the board of a non-profit agency. When I first got the call I wasn't too excited about coaching Joe. I had watched him in action, and he could be brutally indifferent to the feelings of others and intellectually snobbish. All in all, Joe was not a pleasant fellow to be around.

During our first coaching session, Joe started as he frequently did, by intellectualizing everything going on at the government agency in which he worked. He shared with me his analysis (which appeared to be correct) of this person's behavior and that person's motives until I finally asked him to stop. I looked at him and said, "I already know you're a really smart guy. You don't have to prove it to me, but I'm wondering why you have the need to prove it to yourself." Joe stopped dead in his tracks. After a split second of shock, a boyish grin came across his face. It was as if he was caught doing something wrong. "Is it that obvious?" he replied.

Like so many smart people, Joe used his intelligence as a weapon against other people. Growing up smart isn't always easy. In fact, in many public schools, it is more socially acceptable to be developmentally slow than smart. Smart children are often the targets of ridicule and derision by their classmates. Joe's defense mechanism for childhood survival was to keep people at a distance with his carefully chosen, but cutting, words and indifferent attitude. He knew that he could survive using his intelligence, so he did not consider how he affected those around him until his personality caught up with him. He made the mistake of embarrassing his boss's boss with one of his offhand remarks in a meeting, and his intelligence was suddenly no longer the shield that protected him. It was his worst nightmare.

Luckily, Joe turned out to be ripe for coaching. His wife had recently been complaining about the same qualities of which I was making him conscious. His job and his marriage would be in jeopardy if he didn't learn to act differently, win back people he had offended, and avoid making the same mistakes in the future. Joe's coaching plan involved a few simple but specific steps, which he followed religiously.

To begin with, he was coached never to be the first one to speak in meetings. His quick responses often precluded other people from making their points and gave the impression that he was grandstanding. Instead, he was to use the techniques of active listening described in Reason #1, Overlooking the Importance of People, to hear what other people were saying.

The next step was to always tie his own ideas together with the ideas expressed by other people. In other words, he had to seek similarities between his ideas and others' ideas—something that would be impossible to do if he weren't really listening. By seeing similarities he could assure that everyone walked away from a problem-solving session feeling like a winner.

The third coaching hint was to count slowly to three before answering any questions directed to him. This would diminish the appearance of being flip or rash in his comments, give him more time to prepare a thoughtful response, and reduce the inclination toward sarcasm that often accompanied his quicker responses. In the end, his responses might contain the same content, but the moment of hesitation changed the perception of his being a "loose cannon."

Within weeks, Joe changed noticeably. When his boss was called for input about Joe's progress, he said that Joe was like a new man and that the people working with him could see the difference, although they didn't know to what to attribute it. Joe avoided derailment by adding to his skill set and, he tells me tongue in cheek, avoided divorce by practicing the same behaviors at home. Joe approached the coaching hints in much the same way as he approached intellectual challenges—with tenacity and perseverance. He didn't particularly care to know much about why he acted as he did; he only knew that he didn't want to derail and was willing to do whatever it took to avoid it—and he did.

Not all people are as successful as Joe, however, when it comes to matters of character or personality. In contrast, another fellow, George, was advised to get coaching for much the same reason as Joe. In his case, though, he had already been sued for sexual harassment by one of his subordinates. George claimed that all that he did was make some innocent jokes, at which everyone laughed. He was the proverbial bull in a china shop. George was always offending someone with his jokes or casual remarks but never noticed that people didn't like it. Sure they might have laughed, perhaps uncomfortably, at the moment, but people tended to avoid him so that they did not fall victim to his thoughtlessness.

When George was asked why he thought his boss wanted him coached, his reply was that people in his department were overly sensitive, and he supposed he should be more careful. When asked what the value of being more careful might be, he said that it would get his boss off his back. It appeared from the outset that George was not a particularly good candidate for coaching. His inability to see how his behavior affected others, and the lack of desire to correct it for that same reason, made it virtually impossible for George to change. The way he saw it, the rest of the world was against poor, innocent George, a perception that George just couldn't, or wouldn't, overcome. George will spend his life feeling persecuted, never realizing that he and the world interact, and that it is not just the world acting on George. Within a year George was "made redundant" during a corporate downsizing.

George and Joe are representative of the differences between people who respond favorably to coaching and those who don't— people who have the insight to see how their behaviors get in the way of long-term success and people who can't (or won't) admit that their own behaviors play any part in their career difficulties. It appears that 75 percent of the people who are coached are able to make significant changes in their work and their lives as the result of coaching; the other 25 percent do not. It is most likely that if you are still reading this book, you are in the 75 percent category.

Successful behavioral change, especially in the area of character or personality, requires a foundation of emotional stability. People who are so damaged by early childhood experiences that make it impossible for them to see how these experiences affect the present have a difficult time making the *leap of faith* that coaching requires. It is common to hear people express fear about changing. The major fear is that changing certain aspects of one's behavior will cause them to be *less* effective. After all, for the largest portion of their professional lives they have relied on one or two strengths, and now they are being asked to balance those strengths with complementary skills. The request evokes uncertainty and anxiety. It also brings up fears that even a single change will set off a chain of life changes. A strong foundation of emotional stability, however, enables them to have enough faith in the coaching process to at least test out the coaching hints. Absent this foundation, the request for change is just too great.

The Five Most Deadly Character Traits

There are five character traits that most often lead to career derailment. Of course, there may be others, but these are the ones that seem to trip people up most frequently. They include:

- condescension
- abrasiveness
- belligerence
- blaming
- insensitivity

Each one alone is bad enough, but when one person possesses all five traits (and some people do), it's deadly. You may wonder how anyone with all five characteristics could survive for long in an organization. It happens in a number of circumstances. The most common scenario is that the person possesses a unique skill set that is difficult to find or reproduce. The person usually knows this and it only serves to exacerbate the offensive behaviors. He or she has no reason to change because the behavior gets rewarded along with the valued skills. The obvious problem here is that sooner or later someone with the same skills, but not the offensive behavior, comes along and looks mighty attractive to the organization.

A second scenario is that the organizational culture actually *values* the offensive behavior. I once conducted a management skills program for a group like this. It was the sales department of a well-known manufacturing firm, and out of a group of twenty-five participants, twenty of them possessed each of the five deadly character traits. These twenty people would ignore the ground rules that the group set for itself, come to group sessions late, talk over one another, one-up each other, and, in general, act abrasive, belligerent, condescending, and insensitive. When confronted with their behavior, they blamed the other five for not being enough fun! I'd never seen anything like it. When I spoke with the department manager on the lunch break, he actually seemed proud of his team's behavior. He grinned and said that they were on their best behavior. I'd hate to see their worst behavior!

This particular organization isn't alone. There are others where specific, inappropriate behaviors are viewed as simply eccentricities of the company and its employees. Their customers and clients are aware of the behavior, as are candidates applying for jobs and others in their industry. Because of some unusual or special service or product that they provide, they can get away with it. These organizations don't thrive for long, however. The inappropriateness of their actions eventually catches up with them. At some point another company provides the same services but without the offensive behavior.

A good example of an organizational culture that condoned inappropriate behavior is the phone company. When AT&T was the only show in town for long-distance service, customers had to tolerate abrasive and condescending telephone operators. To add insult to injury, their prices were exorbitant. Once deregulation became a fact of life, the story changed. Service has improved and prices have declined in the past decade.

Here are some examples of how the five deadly character traits play out in real life and people who derailed because of them.

Condescension

Condescension is characterized by giving others the feeling that you're placating them or doing them a favor. People who are condescending hold themselves above others due to real or perceived status or privilege. Whether or not they really are of a higher status isn't the point. There are people of the highest social standing who are not condescending and people of the lowest who are.

There is a type of social clustering that occurs in the workplace that reflects the clustering in other circumstances. At work, people who have similar interests will have lunch together or do social things together. However, if common courtesy is not extended to those outside the group due to status, sex, race, ethnicity, or some other subjective variable, clustering becomes condescension. People who avoid derailment are the ones who treat the janitor with the same dignity and respect they offer to the company president. These are the people who really see the service people around them and believe that there are no worthless jobs or people.

It is difficult to know how people who have very public lives act in private, but we do get a feeling for how they might act based on their public personas. Whether or not she actually was, Princess Grace gave the impression that she was not the least bit condescending, whereas Prince Charles gives quite the opposite impression. Princess Grace was, by all accounts, revered by the people of Monaco. Prince Charles, on the other hand, has done little to endear himself to the populace of Great Britain. If anything, in the midst of his marital problems, public opinion favored his wife, Princess Diana, in no small part due to his condescending manner and her publicly (at least) warm ways.

Abrasiveness

Abrasive behaviors involve acting out against other people. Whereas condescending people are, at times, passive-aggressive (appearing benign on the surface, but subversively acting in their own best interest), abrasive people are just plain aggressive. Newt Gingrich provides an outstanding model for the term *abrasive*. Regardless of the value or content of his message, it is difficult to hear because it is couched in so much negativity about the opposing political party. His comments about the Democrats, whether on target or not, come across as snide remarks rather than logical, albeit critical, assessments. His behavior might also fall into the condescending category because he frequently smirks, which suggests an air of superiority or imperiousness, while he makes his abrasive remarks.

A notable business figure with an abrasive personality is hotelier Leona Helmsley. In the midst of legal problems that resulted from her failure to pay sufficient taxes, Helmsley managed to alienate a rather substantial population of would-be guests with her comment that only the "little people" pay taxes. Throughout her trial similar thoughtless and abrasive remarks (always devoid of remorse) only contributed further to her ultimate incarceration for tax evasion.

Abrasive people care more about the content of their messages and less about the impact that the messages will have on others. They choose "hard" words to get the point across rather than neutral ones. Hard words are ones that offend or attack, whereas neutral ones lean toward bridging differences of opinion and problem solving. Hard words are frequently value-laden, whereas neutral ones are more objective. The differences sound something like this:

Hard: *It's obvious that you simply didn't put the time into writing the report that it required. If you had, it wouldn't have turned out so ineptly written and blatantly filled with mistakes.*

Neutral: *The report isn't what I had anticipated. It contains numerous errors of fact and grammar. I'm wondering whether the time required to do it was actually devoted to it?*

You will note that the neutral statement did not attack or condemn, but rather presented a simple statement of fact. Additionally, the hard word choices include "you" statements, as opposed to "I" statements, that tend to make another person defensive and less likely to want to work through the problem.

Belligerence

Barry Scheck, one of the trial lawyers for O. J. Simpson, is a good example of someone who is belligerent. His questions were verbal blows. Judge Lance Ito had to shout at him to get him to listen. Scheck was argumentative and bullying. One might say that he was just doing his job, which was to defend Simpson to the best of his ability; however, all of us could use the same excuse in our jobs, albeit with less dire consequences, and it would still not make belligerent behavior acceptable.

Another public personality whose behavior borders on being belligerent is Ross Perot. His ideas are often lost in the manner in which he expresses them. Much of the time he comes across as angry and abusive. At times, his nonverbal behavior is inappropriate to the situation. You can tell that he's uncomfortable when he delivers a scathing message with a smile on his face. Like Scheck and other belligerent people, Perot is a verbal bully. He has a good command of the language and uses it as a weapon against others. People often say that they like his ideas, but not the man.

Blaming

Most of us have had the great displeasure of working with a blaming or Teflon boss or coworker. When something goes wrong, watch out because someone is going to wind up the scapegoat. Their inability to admit their own mistakes goes beyond any single mistake; it is at the very core of their interactions with others. People who are unable to admit mistakes are frequently the very same people who lack insight into their own behavior.

Oliver North provides us with a glimpse into the behavior of the blamer. When the Iran-contra debacle began in 1986, North was the deputy director of political affairs for the National Security Council. Once again, television cameras provided us with an indelible image of the event and of Lieutenant Colonel North during the Iran-contra hearings. As he blamed others for the events that took place, the cameras captured a handsome, articulate, and seemingly sincere civil servant. Through it all, North displayed a cavalier attitude.

When he was dismissed and later indicted for the role he played in carrying out a plan to sell arms to Iran, he blamed everyone except himself. He claimed that his actions were fully authorized by his superiors. Despite this finger pointing, in May of 1989 a jury convicted North of obstructing Congress and destroying documents. Incredibly, the charges were later dropped or overturned. Even more astonishing was his decision to run as the Republican candidate for the U.S. Senate in Virginia in 1994. As usual, the blamer cannot see that he has done any wrong and, in this case, has the audacity to run for public office following what others would perceive to be public humiliation.

Insensitivity

Insensitive people tend to disregard others' preferences or desires, embarrass others with thoughtless comments, and make certain that their own needs prevail. They frequently speak before they think, thereby saying things that in retrospect they wish they hadn't—but the damage is already done.

Former Dodger manager Al Campanis derailed a number of years back due to his insensitivity. Campanis's forty-six-year career with the Dodgers came to a screeching halt in 1987 with one insensitive remark. In response to a question posed by Ted Koppel in a *Nightline* interview about why there were so few black managers and owners in baseball, he said, "I truly believe that they [blacks] may not have some of the necessities to be, let's say, a field manager, or perhaps a general manager." Campanis derailed following this statement, vowing to the very end that he had been misunderstood. Perhaps he had been misunderstood, but the comment speaks for itself. It is what makes thinking before speaking so important.

Insensitivity isn't always thoughtless—at times it is an intentionally used tactical weapon. One woman in a workshop on interpersonal skills spent the first day embarrassing and berating others. To a grossly overweight woman she made the comment, "The food here [at the conference center] is so heavy. I must have gained ten pounds. I feel like a beached whale." During an evening of group singing and dancing, she stood up and mimicked another participant who had a heavy Asian accent and who had just led the group in a song. When I asked to speak with her privately to give her some feedback about how she was affecting the rest of the group members, she proudly admitted that she could find a person's Achilles' heel and go after it. She told me that this was her way of maintaining a competitive edge.

Insensitivity, whether intentional or otherwise, gives the impression that you are a loose cannon. People who are insensitive are frequently excluded from important client or customer meetings for fear of what they're going to say. Insensitive people wind up being avoided in the workplace because their coworkers don't particularly care to set themselves up for hurt or embarrassment. Failing to know how you affect others, being unaware that you may have hurt someone else, and neglecting to ask for feedback about your behavior are other examples of insensitivity, which may also be viewed as *lacking insight*. People who lack insight have huge blind spots about their own personalities because they are largely oblivious to how others respond to them. They fail to see the reactions of others because they are so absorbed in themselves. Lack of insight probably causes more career derailments than any other single factor.

William Agee, former CEO of Bendix Corporation, and more recently of Morrison Knudsen, provides us with an example of someone who derailed for, among other things, lacking insight. Agee, an honors graduate of Harvard, was chief financial officer at

Boise Cascade by the time he was thirty-one and CEO at Bendix by thirty-eight. People expected great things from him and he didn't let them down.

The beginning of his derailment process began amid controversy when he was at Bendix that he was having an affair with his young executive assistant, Mary Cunningham. Although he denied the rumors, resentment against both Cunningham and Agee for his preferential treatment of her reflected poorly on his judgment. His judgment was called into question even more so when he married her. Although his business decisions certainly played a major role in his ultimate departure from Bendix, it appeared that his lack of insight about how his behavior affected others deprived him of the support from staff and management that he might otherwise have had.

What might have eventually been overlooked as simply a matter of the heart was later revisited when the pair found themselves in trouble again, this time at Morrison Knudsen. Not having learned his lesson about preferential treatment, Agee this time put his wife at the helm of the Morrison Knudsen Foundation. His attempts to turn around the declining company met with resistance as he alienated employees with his insensitive management style. Top that off with the fact that members of the community found both Agee and Cunningham standoffish and pretentious and their dismissal was inevitable.

When Too Much of a Good Thing Is a Good Thing

There are five behaviors that counter the deadly character traits: kindness, honesty, humility, genuineness, and self-awareness. Remember, when you are trying to overcome your strengths it is not particularly helpful to think about *stopping* a behavior. You only focus more on the behavior that you want most to diminish! You must add new skills to your existing repertoire. Add these five, and your personality worries will be over.

Kindness

Many of us grew up with the Golden Rule: *Do unto others as you would have others do unto you*. True kindness takes that motto a step further. In order to be truly kind, you must now *treat others as they would like to be treated*. I've already described the importance of seeing people for who they are. In order to be kind, you must now respond to who *they* are and what *they* would like, not who *you* are and what *you* would like.

Many of the behaviors inherent to kindness overlap with the relationship-building behaviors described under Reason #1. Kindness goes beyond relationship building, however, because it also encompasses what you do when there is no quid pro quo, when you have nothing to gain from the act. This concept is exemplified in the role played by Kevin Costner in the movie *The War*.

In one scene he takes the cotton candy he has just purchased for his wife and daughter at a fair and gives it to some bullies who have been beating up on his kids. When his son looks at him incredulously and asks why he did that, his response is simple: "Because it looks like they haven't been given nothing in a long time." This type of kindness stems from a sort of generosity—not a generosity of materialism, but a generosity of spirit. You are kind not because someone reminds you to be, or because you know that you will gain something tangible from it, but because you want to make a difference in the lives of those around you—even those whom you may never see again.

I can remember the exact moment in childhood when I learned my first lesson in kindness. It was on a crowded subway in Manhattan when I was five or six years old. My aunt had taken me to see her office in the city and we were returning home amid the rush-hour commuters who were packed like sardines into the train. I watched as a young professional woman stood, tapped an elderly woman on the shoulder, and motioned her to the seat she had just vacated. The older woman sat down wearily and the younger woman remained standing until she exited many stops later. A simple act of kindness that took place nearly forty years ago had such a profound effect on me that to this day I recall it nearly every time I ride the subway.

Honesty

Honesty can be looked at in a number of ways. Do you tell the truth when asked a question, or do you pass the buck and look for someone else to blame? Do you give people honest feedback, or do you say what you think people want to hear? Are you willing to speak the unspoken—even when not asked—or are you content to not rock the boat? No matter how you slice it, honesty involves having the integrity to say and do the right thing no matter how difficult.

When it comes to speaking your mind, there are different ways of being honest. It is possible to be honest without demolishing another person. Honesty does not always have to be hurtful, but it does have to meet two criteria: it must be direct and it must be kind. Once, after a lengthy explanation in the ways of being honest, someone in a workshop summarized it beautifully when she pointed out that *honesty is the ability to tell someone to go to hell so that they look forward to the trip!* Let's take a look at how you might successfully meet this challenge.

Quite often, when people are coached to be honest but with kindness, they think that they are being asked to act passively—to care more about the receiver of the message than about making their points. This is far from the case. It is just that people who are brutally honest frequently go out of bounds in terms of their direct, straightforward behavior. It becomes too much of a good thing. By following these "three Ds" of honesty, you will increase the likelihood of getting your message across without damaging the relationship:

DESCRIBE   = Describe why you are having the conversation with this person.

DISCUSS   = Discuss the situation, using active listening to fully understand the other person's position or opinion.

DETERMINE = Determine outcomes suitable for both parties involved.

All too often honesty comes out sounding something like this:

Bill, I can't believe that report you gave me last week. You must have been asleep when you prepared it. You made mistakes about the size of the workforce and surrounding population. You even misspelled the CEO's name. You can certainly do better than that.

Messages that sound like this one, no matter how true they are, do nothing to further the relationship, build self-esteem, or encourage creative problem solving. The receiver of this message winds up feeling small and stupid. Notice that by using the three Ds and avoiding blame through the use of the word *you,* the entire tone is turned around, even though the sentiment remains the same:

DESCRIBE

Speaker: *Bill, I'd like to talk to you about the report that you handed in last week. Is this a good time?*
Receiver: *Sure.*

DISCUSS

Speaker: *I noticed that, in addition to being late, it had numerous errors in both content and typing. I was wondering what happened.*

This doesn't seem like the quality of work that you're capable of doing.

Receiver: *Well, actually, I did it in kind of a rush and didn't have time to proof it before I gave it to you.*

Speaker: *What made you so rushed?*

Receiver: *The equipment that I needed to access the data was down for nearly a week. We couldn't get anyone out here to fix it.*

Speaker: *Why didn't I know about it?*

Receiver: *You've been so busy with the new acquisition that I didn't want to bother you.*

Speaker: *I'm sorry that you felt like you couldn't come to me. It has really put me on the spot. Was there something that I could have done differently that would have made you more comfortable to let me know?*

Receiver: *No, not really. I guess I just didn't want to burden you any further than you already were.*

DETERMINE

Speaker: *I appreciate your trying to protect me like that, but it has created a problem for me. What is most important now is to decide what to do to prevent this from happening again. I need to know when I assign something to you that I'll get it on time and that it'll be free from so many errors.*

Receiver: *I'm sorry that I put you in this position. In the future, I'll let you know whether there are any extenuating circumstances that prohibit me from getting my assignments to you on time.*

Speaker: *Good. That's what I need. Thanks for your cooperation.*

Following the three Ds allows you to be direct and kind at the same time. The message is the same in both of the examples above, but the second scenario will assure long-term cooperation and goodwill.

Humility

Humility is embodied in this paraphrase of Vince Lombardi's coaching philosophy:

When the team loses—it's my fault.
When the team does well—we did it together.
When the team wins—they did it themselves.

Humility is the absence of arrogance and the presence of modesty. It is the ability to put your own achievements into a perspective that simultaneously recognizes your own limitations and the strengths of others. Humble people do not boast or require extended time in the limelight (we all need a bit). They are so self-assured that they internalize their strengths and use them as stepping-stones for future success.

One example of someone who lacks humility is financier Donald Trump. Not only does Trump exaggerate his accomplishments, but he diminishes others in the process. A number of years ago Trump took over construction of Central Park's ice skating rink from the city of New York. When the project was completed, he called a press conference to gloat over the fact that he had succeeded where the city had failed. When asked how he managed to finish the project under budget and on time, he could have acknowledged the work of good contractors and associates, but instead Trump chose to use the opportunity to demean Mayor Ed Koch and otherwise impugn the reputation of the city.

General Norman Schwarzkopf, in contrast, exemplifies a man of humility. Despite the fact that he was instrumental in the decisive defeat of the Iraqi military during Operation Desert Storm, Schwarzkopf never took the credit for himself alone. He shared the triumph with his colleagues and troops, and, in the process, allowed everyone involved to be a hero. It's easy to see why a man like Schwarzkopf is revered while in the minds of many someone like Trump is viewed as a caricature of himself.

Ironically, those who are unable to be humble are often raised as children in households so withholding of praise and affirmation that the child must call attention to himself or herself or otherwise fade into oblivion. The behaviors that we learned to survive difficult childhoods later become the cause of derailment. Self-confident people are able to highlight their accomplishments discreetly for the purpose of furthering their goals; people lacking humility must showcase their strengths as if their lives depended on it—because they do.

It is not as if humble people don't know that they are good—or even great. They do know this, but they lack the need to receive constant praise for it. Humility should not be confused with passivity. They are two entirely different things. Whereas passivity is marked by the unwillingness or inability to be proactive, humility is characterized by the desire to downplay one's position, strengths, or contributions.

Genuineness

Being comfortable with ourselves as imperfect humans—scars, flaws, and all—is the essence of being genuine. It is not quite the same as the expression *what you see is what you get,* because implied in that maxim may be a take-it-or-leave-it attitude. It's more like *I'm not perfect, but I know that I'm not and I don't try to be anyone other than who I am.* Genuine people accept who they are, and are likely to accept others for who they are for the same reason. They can laugh at their own foibles and eccentricities without embarrassment or self-consciousness. They have relinquished the need to be perfect.

The opposite of genuineness is pretention—putting on airs or pretending to be who you are not. I knew a man once who was al-

ways showing excessive kindness to others that had nothing what-
soever to do with the recipient's needs or circumstances. One
Christmas he gave each member of his staff a piece of silver from
Tiffany's, a seemingly kind and generous gesture on the surface.
The only problem was that this same man refused to give performance reviews, say a kind word about anyone, or provide even
cost-of-living increases to his employees when they were warranted. His staff would have much preferred to be recognized for
their performance throughout the year than rewarded with an ex-
travagant gift once a year. Similarly, he would take them to the
most expensive restaurants in Chicago for their birthdays but failed
to say good morning to them. It was more important to him that
he appear magnanimous than that he be genuine. And, in turn, he
got *subversive compliance* from his staff. They would do only what
was necessary to keep afloat in their positions and nothing more.

Self-Awareness

People who are self-aware know their strengths and flaws and act
to improve their skills. They are aware of the effect they have on
others. Combined with genuineness, honesty, and humility, self-
awareness enables individuals to respond flexibly to different situations.

Self-awareness can be developed in a number of ways.

1. **ASK FOR FEEDBACK.** Even if there's no formal mechanism
in place for it at your job, ask other people for feedback. Couch it
in terms of what they think you could do more of, less of, or continue. This model provides a nonthreatening way of giving, and
receiving, feedback. If you ask for feedback, however, be sure that
you're ready to hear it. Once given, don't argue with it or try to
explain away your behavior. The best way to deal with feedback is
to ask for clarification if you don't understand it, thank the giver,

and then go off to think about it. Even if it's only one person's opinion, you need to consider the ramifications of the feedback and how many more people may be thinking the exact same thing but not telling you.

2. **USE A 360° FEEDBACK INSTRUMENT,** a performance survey available to all levels of employees—professionals, supervisors, managers, and senior executives. The surveys are completed anonymously by people who know your work and returned to a third party, who then sends them off for computer processing, from which a computer profile of your strengths and needs for development emerges. In Resources you'll find the name of a reliable company that you can contact for such profiles. Because the results can at times be pretty overwhelming, it is recommended that a feedback instrument be used in conjunction with a business coach. You'll find coaching contacts listed in Resources as well.

3. **TAKE SELF-AWARENESS CLASSES.** These classes focus on behavior in a business context. Unlike EST or Wellspring, they're typically designed for businesspeople who want to examine how their behavior impedes or contributes to career success. The company I consider to be the nation's premier provider of such classes is NTL (National Training Laboratory). They've been facilitating self-awareness programs for businesspeople for nearly fifty years. You'll find a contact for them, as well as other reputable organizations, in Resources.

4. **GET A BUSINESS COACH.** Good coaches work with you to overcome specific behaviors that may contribute to potential derailment. In addition to providing you with coaching hints related to your particular situation, they can refer you to other resources in your community that may be helpful for assuring ongoing self-awareness. Many use 360° feedback instruments as part of the coaching process.

5. **ENTER INTO COUNSELING.** At times, behaviors are so ingrained and related to early childhood experiences that longer-

term, in-depth professional help is required to understand and change them. Since I am a licensed psychotherapist myself, I offer this recommendation with somewhat of a bias, but even coaches with no psychological backgrounds report that from 75 to 90 percent of the people they coach are referred to counseling for treatment that goes beyond the scope of coaching.

Avoid Going for the Bait

A client I've been coaching called to tell me about a situation that he thought he handled poorly. We had been working on how to overcome the impression that others have of him of being too blunt, undiplomatic, and hurtful in his remarks to others. We discussed many of the coaching hints already provided in this chapter, and he was making some headway in winning back the regard of his staff and colleagues. He slid backward, however, when someone did the same thing to him that he was accused of doing to others.

A female coworker sent him an E-mail message berating him for being rude, slow in responding to requests, and mean-spirited at meetings. She sent it not only to him, but electronically copied all of the people reporting to him and to his boss. Furious, he responded in kind with an equally abusive letter in which he let the woman know what he thought of her. In short, he went for the bait. The woman who sent the letter wanted to get a rise out of him, and she did. The situation was now escalating, and both parties looked childish.

One technique to avoid matching the inappropriate intensity level of another person, and thereby avoid going for the bait, is called *fogging*. Although the man and I had discussed it during his coaching sessions, the importance of fogging was underscored by this encounter. Fogging is especially helpful when someone catches you unaware or off guard with their intensity or anxiety.

When others are angry or abusive it is human nature to become angry and abusive back. Meeting the other person's intensity level typically only escalates a problem.

Fogging involves first putting up a visual fog between you and the other person so that his or her intensity is diffused and neither intimidates nor infuriates you. Next, you attempt to de-escalate the situation by remaining calm and using specific phrases designed to permit you to maintain your dignity and allow others to maintain theirs. Phrases like "I can see you are really upset by this. Let me check into it and get back to you" or "I had no idea you felt this way. Tell me more about it" are examples of fogging that buy you time to gather your composure or investigate the complaint, without responding in kind.

When the man asked what he could have done differently, it was suggested that he might have responded with a return E-mail message that said: *I had no idea that my behavior is being interpreted in the way that you described. Why don't we schedule a meeting within the next few days to sit down and discuss the problem so that we can remedy it as quickly as possible.* He said that this was all well and good, except that it didn't address the fact that he was embarrassed in front of his staff and boss. *His* response, on the other hand, evened the score, a fact about which he appeared to be proud.

As was explained to him, there are any number of ways of winning a battle without losing the war. The preferred response would go a long way toward assuring his ongoing success despite how his colleague chose to act. By smoothing the waters, he would allow others to see that even when provoked, he treats people with dignity and respect. He would wind up looking like a hero, rather than being seen as stooping to his colleague's level. In keeping with Lao-tzu's teaching "Fail to honor people, they fail to honor you," honoring others over the long tenure of your career will always serve you better than acting out of malice or vindictiveness.

S trategies for Crafting a Winning Personality: Interacting with Others

1. Never embarrass anyone—ever.
2. Don't tell jokes at the expense of anyone except yourself (and think twice before you do that).
3. Publicly praise, privately criticize.
4. Know when to give up the battle so that you can win the war.
5. Remember to say please and thank you.
6. Create win-win situations by considering everyone's needs, not just your own.
7. Find ways to allow people to save face—give the benefit of the doubt.
8. Be humble.
9. Be a gracious loser—and winner.
10. Be assertive (not aggressive).
11. Give other people credit when it's due (and maybe even when it's not).
12. Be honest, but be careful how you express your honesty.
13. Look people in the eye when you speak with them.
14. Stop what you are doing and pay attention to people when they come into your office.
15. Think before you speak—especially when you are angry or upset.
16. Use the lowest level of muscle possible.
17. Despite how you are treated, always treat others with dignity and respect.

S trategies for Crafting a Winning Personality: Self-Development

18. Use a 360° feedback instrument to get input into how others perceive you.

19. Attend NTL's Human Interaction Laboratory (see page 239).

20. Attend an assertive communications class.

21. Be kind to yourself—so that you can be kind to others.

22. Be who you are, but be the best you possible.

23. Take self-awareness classes.

24. Use the three Ds of honesty: *describe* your concern, *discuss* the problem, *determine* outcomes.

Difficulty Working with Authority

LEARN HOW TO MANAGE UP

A seldom-discussed fact of business life is the need to "manage up." The concept of managing up is not to be confused with toadying or apple polishing. I'm not suggesting that you act insincere or in a way calculated to garner favor from management. *Managing up* means that you are aware of the need to cultivate a relationship with management that produces satisfactory results for *both* parties. Managing up simply means that you understand the unspoken quid pro quo between you and your boss and consciously make an effort to keep up your end of the agreement.

People rarely refer to the men and women who supervise their work or to whom they report as "bosses." Instead, they call them leaders, facilitators, coaches, coordinators, and an array of other nonhierarchical terms in an effort to remove the traditional notion that one position is in any way more important or better than another. After all, if there is a *subordinate* then there must be a *superior*. Modern theories of motivation suggest that in order to bring out the best in people managers can no longer rely on the power of their positions, but must build relationships of mutual respect. Unlike their predecessors, who saluted authority figures simply for the authority of power they possessed, today's workers expect to actually have a relationship with their supervisors, and the new terminology is reflective of this change.

Nevertheless, a rose is still a rose, and a boss is still a boss, and here's where the necessity for *managing up* comes in. No matter what you call the boss, the fact remains that most people working in companies and organizations report to someone else who reviews their work and makes determinations about salary, promotion, assignments, and, at times, termination. You can change the term used to describe him or her, you can expect to have an amiable relationship with him or her, but you can't alter the fact that you are ultimately accountable to someone higher in the organization. From an entry-level position right on up to the CEO, everyone is accountable to someone. People who successfully avoid premature career derailment understand that, as with all other relationships, this relationship must be managed effectively.

Although the labels have become fuzzier and management techniques friendlier, the nature of the employer/employee relationship has not changed significantly. Labor attorneys are as busy as ever representing companies for their decisions to terminate employees and employees who believe they have been unjustly treated. The fact remains that you have to satisfy the expectations of the people who supervise you if you are to succeed in the workplace.

Managing up is difficult in the new employment arena because no other workplace relationship resembles one's original family experience as much as the employee-manager relationship. For the employee, this relationship may encompass all of the same frustrations, triumphs, challenges, and satisfaction that existed within the relationship with his or her father, mother, or other primary caretaker. An employee may unwittingly respond to the boss in much the same way he or she responded to the first of life's authority figures.

Because of this association between caretakers and bosses, employees' responses may vary between extraordinarily tolerant in the worst of situations, and intolerant in the best of situations. This creates a unique dilemma because derailment can come from being too submissive as well as from being too argumentative or unwilling to comply with directions. The real trick is to know (1) what the boss expects from you and (2) how to maintain your integrity as you walk the fine line between being a yes-person and being a thorn in the boss's side.

Perhaps this checklist is a place to begin thinking about how well you work with authority figures.

_____ I am able to disagree with the boss when I feel strongly about something.

_____ I see it as my duty to provide the boss with alternative viewpoints.

_____ I would rate myself high on being able to disagree without being disagreeable.

_____ I know when to disagree with the boss and when not to.

_____ I balance respect for authority with voicing a dissenting viewpoint.

_____ I know what kind of boss will listen to a differing viewpoint and which will not and act accordingly.

_____ I would never be accused of currying favor with someone in order to advance myself.

_____ I would never be accused of defying authority.

_____ I have worked through whatever issues I may have had with the type of parenting I received (either positive or negative).

_____ I am able to objectively assess my boss's strengths and developmental areas.

_____ I know when someone in authority is being unreasonable with me, and I don't usually take it personally.

_____ I see people in authority as only human.

An interesting coaching case that portrays the effect of parenting on the boss/employee relationship involved a woman, whom I'll call Carolyn. She requested coaching as a means of helping her to manage work stress. Carolyn was clearly an upwardly mobile career woman who seemed to have all the skills needed to be successful within her current organization or any other organization to which she might move. She had a good career track record with other companies and was articulate, intelligent, poised, and self-confident. Coincidentally, I knew her boss from some consulting that I had done for their company a number of years before. My recollection of him was that he was sarcastic, sexist, and a know-it-all. He saw himself as "the boss" and everyone else as merely underlings.

Throughout the first coaching session, I couldn't quite figure out what the real problem was. Carolyn never mentioned her boss (an omission I found strange), only that her job was very demanding and creating an abundance of stress for her. Without revealing my own assessment of her boss, I finally asked about her relationship with him. She skirted the issue for several minutes, and each time I gently came back to the topic. Suddenly, Carolyn started sobbing. As it turned out, she was feeling inadequate and incompetent. No matter what she did, her boss wasn't satisfied. Carolyn was certain that it was all her fault.

After exploring the situation with her a bit more, I turned the topic to her personal life. Was she married? Were her parents still alive? Did she have siblings? With this, she lit up. No, she wasn't married, but she did have a particularly close relationship with her parents. She had grown up an only child, doted on adoring grandparents and aunts. She thought that she probably wasn't married yet because no man could measure up to her father, whom she described as a loving, considerate, and nurturing man.

Carolyn's greatest strengths—her self-confidence and talent—were now put in question by a boss who was the polar opposite of her father. Carolyn came to the job seeing the boss as her loving mother, nurturing father, and doting extended family all rolled into one. Despite all factors pointing to the contrary, she believed in the boss more than she believed in herself. She was not capable of seeing the boss for who he really was and, therefore, bought into his critical assessment of her. Her perception was that he was the all-knowing, benevolent father figure. There couldn't possibly be anything wrong with him, so it had to be her!

Subsequent coaching sessions with Carolyn focused on enabling her to assess her boss's behaviors critically vis-à-vis her own and to deal with those behaviors more objectively. She was ultimately able to separate the boss from her father in her mind, and when she did, she made the decision to find a boss who was in actuality more like her father. Carolyn realized that there were certainly some areas on which she needed to work, but that it would be better for her to leave the company. She is now happily working for a small company in Indiana that has a family-like feel to it. She vows never again to let someone take away her self-esteem.

As for Carolyn's former boss—he's an example of someone who manages up well. His own boss is a lot like him and, in fact, appreciates and rewards his hard-nosed approach to management. Both former marines, they remain true to the marine motto *semper fidelis*—always loyal. The man is still with the company, making people's lives miserable, and no one in authority seems to be taking notice.

The opposite phenomenon—total acquiescence to the boss—can be equally damaging to one's career. A manager once asked if I would work with one of his employees. The manager's main complaint was that the employee, Dave, would never challenge anything he said. Dave would follow the boss's instructions to the letter, even if it became apparent in the process that there was a better way to do it or a more appropriate path to pursue. The particular behavior that frustrated the manager was just part of a larger problem. Someone who won't challenge authority often won't take the kinds of risks needed to explore, make mistakes, learn from those mistakes, and go on to bigger and better things. As a member of a creative services team, Dave was *expected* to take risks.

Dave's greatest strength was following instructions. He grew up in an Eastern culture where respect for authority was demonstrated by close adherence to the directions and desires of the elders. Like Carolyn, Dave had to learn to separate his early experience with authority from the business situation with the boss. His coaching sessions involved enabling him to think and act independently of his boss's desires. He was coached first to develop a weekly plan for task accomplishment that included two to three items that he could see were needed in the department but that weren't mentioned by his boss. Next, he was instructed to give his own opinion at least once at every staff meeting. The third thing he was coached to do was to speak more loudly. His quiet, somewhat flat tone of voice gave others the perception that he was someone who could be walked on. The combined coaching hints—to think more broadly, give his own opinions, and do so in a louder voice—were designed to eventually increase his self-confidence. Once this happened, he would be more likely to take more risks. The goal was to get Dave to "walk the walk" and "talk the talk." Fortunately, Dave had a boss who was very supportive of the process and not only allowed but also encouraged him to overcome his particular strengths.

The My Lai Massacre: A Study in Deference to Authority

There is no better example of someone on the compliant side of the managing-up spectrum than that of Lieutenant William Calley Jr. In 1968 the Vietnam War was raging. Calley was in charge of a platoon that, on March 16 of the same year, was instructed to invade and destroy the Vietnamese village of My Lai, an alleged Viet Cong stronghold. When they arrived, they found no Viet Cong, but Calley and his platoon nevertheless slaughtered hundreds of innocent civilian women and children.

A fellow soldier was so disturbed by the events that he wrote letters to Congress—letters that eventually brought Calley to trial for murder and resulted in his conviction. Calley's only defense throughout the trial was that he was simply following the instructions of his superiors. His remarks at the time were, "Personally, I didn't kill any Vietnamese that day. I mean personally. I represented the United States of America. My country." These words underscore what happens when one is blindly loyal to authority.

A glimpse into his childhood gives us a few clues to help understand his actions. Calley is described as an unexceptional child and a product of a 1950s upbringing. He was sent to the Florida Military Academy after being caught cheating on a test in the seventh grade. One can only imagine what possessed his family to send him away and what he learned about following instructions once at the academy. One man recalls young Calley being a loyal friend: "[H]is sense of loyalty was wonderful. If you had a problem at 3:30 in the morning he would be there for you." After dropping out of junior college he wandered from job to job until he wound up in the military. The same friend claims that Calley liked the regimentation and needed the discipline that the service afforded.

What he must certainly have learned at the military academy about compliance, especially after being sent there for cheating on a test, combined with the comment about his loyalty to friends, provides us with the greatest insight into his decision to follow the instructions he was given on March 16, 1968. Although Calley's strengths lay in these two factors, they became his greatest liabilities and forever changed his life. After his release from prison (most of which, at President Richard Nixon's direction, was spent in his own apartment under house arrest) after serving less than four years of a life sentence, he refused to talk about the incident and until this day will not give interviews or discuss the matter. His silence is testament to his loyalty to the service, despite the fact that he was the only person convicted of crimes related to what we now call the My Lai Massacre.

Except for the gross atrocities of his crime, Lieutenant Calley is no different from the scores of businesspeople who salute the boss and fail to add value to their positions due to their inability to confront authority when necessary or appropriate. These men and women are great followers, but the company suffers from their unwillingness to think and act independently of authority. They do as they are told, keep their noses clean, and perpetuate the status quo of their organizations.

Frank Biondi and Viacom

The story of the abrupt and surprising dismissal of Frank Biondi as CEO of entertainment giant Viacom, Inc., by his boss, chair Sumner Redstone, illustrates what can happen when a good relationship turns sour. Industry insiders say that the relationship between the two—who were initially viewed as a winning executive team—may have slowly eroded over differences in style and strategy. Just two weeks prior to the dismissal, Biondi attended a fete in honor of Redstone and sang his boss's praises. Similarly, for years Redstone publicly acknowledged Biondi's contributions to Viacom. Behind the scenes, however, a different scenario was being played out.

Redstone hired Biondi in 1987 to help him manage the company that was burdened with a debt ten times its cash flow. Together, the team whittled away the debt and expanded operations. It was widely recognized that Biondi and Redstone didn't always see eye to eye, although little was made of it at the time. Biondi was the Harvard MBA numbers man, while Redstone was the visionary who operated from instinct—a potentially lethal combination unless both parties are aware of the quid pro quo. One incident that underscores their different approaches took place in the late eighties, when on a Friday they made the decision to buy King World. By Monday morning Redstone decided he wanted out of the deal. When Biondi asked why, Redstone said that after consulting with longtime friend Barry Diller, he decided it wasn't viable. Biondi then implied that Redstone's friend might not be the most objective person with whom to consult, since he could be negatively affected by the acquisition. The deal never went through.

There were other occasions when Biondi publicly contradicted Redstone. One such incident was when Redstone declared that acquiring a music company would be "another enormous source of software" while Biondi publicly stated that it was an "awfully small business." Some say that the real turning point came in 1993 when Redstone wanted to buy Paramount and Biondi resisted, insisting that it would overleverage the company's assets. Immediately following this event Redstone became increasingly critical of Biondi, implying that the failure of a costly Paramount film was due to Biondi's negligence. Biondi's influence dwindled to the point where his input into decisions was second-guessed by other Viacom executives who were supported behind the scenes by Redstone, and he was summarily dismissed. In the end, it appears that Biondi's greatest strength, a logical, level-headed approach to managing a business, became his greatest liability, absent the ability to manage up effectively.

Calley and Biondi, both devoted to their careers, are on opposite ends of the managing-up spectrum. Whereas one had difficulty critically assessing the decisions of his superiors, the other did so too much. The secret of successfully managing up is to be willing to take risks with regard to questioning authority, but to know when and how to do it.

Putting the Past into Perspective

Beyond the examples above, difficulties with authority affect the lives of employees in all milieus. A woman called Alice illuminates this phenomenon in a less spectacular setting. The case study is from psychotherapist and corporate coach Susan Picascia. Susan, formerly with the Employee Assistance Program at Cedars Sinai Hospital in Los Angeles, now has her own consulting firm in which she coaches people on how to overcome the effects of childhood experiences in the workplace. She shares with us her experience coaching Alice, the manager of information research at a high-profile, Hollywood-based entertainment firm.

As a manager, Alice is a technically proficient relationship builder who shows respect to her peers and staff and receives the same in return. She prides herself on being a compassionate, people-oriented manager with strong technical skills. Although she works independently in relation to others, Alice becomes dependent in relation to her boss, Curtis.

Unfortunately, Curtis reminds Alice of her father, who was a perfectionist and hypercritical. In Curtis's case, it isn't so much that he's a perfectionist, but rather that he is so self-absorbed that he never takes time to notice Alice's many achievements or to give her feedback—except for negative comments on rare occasions when something isn't done as he wanted it. At those times, Alice cries in private because she feels like she can never do anything right in his eyes. In front of him, she becomes defensive, to which he reacts by saying, "Don't get your back up." She is beginning to question her ability and competence, despite the fact that she has successfully worked with bosses in other firms.

Although this is the first time in her career that Alice has experienced a situation like this one, it certainly won't be the last. The personal development that Alice must now undertake in order to avoid derailment involves developing the ability to put "little Alice" on hold while "adult Alice" takes over. She must learn to judge herself, rather than allowing the opinions of others to eclipse her self-esteem. She can successfully accomplish this with these three specific coaching hints.

1. **LOWER HER ANTENNAE FOR TUNING INTO FEELINGS—** both her feelings and Curtis's. As a result of her experience with her father, Alice is supersensitive to criticism, especially from men. Whereas others would take Curtis's feedback at face value, Alice interprets it as failure. She learned early in life to put extra effort into doing things perfectly in order to ward off potential criticism and has transferred this behavior to the workplace. The obvious problem is that it's impossible to ward off criticism entirely. Inevitably, we all do something differently than the boss wants it done and we must make adjustments. Alice's need to be perfect is getting in her way. No one in her present life—not even Curtis—expects her to be perfect. She must let go of this particular childhood defense mechanism and become less sensitive to Curtis's requests for change, as well as the manner in which he delivers these messages.

2. **RAISE HER ANTENNAE FOR MESSAGE CONTENT.** Conversely, Alice should pay more attention to the content of the mes-

sage, thereby avoiding overreaction to how it is delivered. By focusing on the content, she can remove herself from the role of the child who is responsible for the opinions of her father/boss.

3. **USE POSITIVE SELF-TALK AND VISUALIZE SUCCESS.** When feelings from the past surface, Alice must say to herself, "I will attend to my feelings later, right now the focus is on content. I will respond to content in an open-minded, nondefensive way." Self-talk is a powerful tool to tape over the old messages that play in the back of our heads. By using self-talk and by visualizing successful encounters with the boss, Alice can develop new messages and images on which she can rely for support and encouragement when they are needed most.

Alice permits her past to define her present and future. The work of each of us is to be able to objectively see the authority figures in our lives as they really are and not as ghosts from the past. If you find yourself overreacting to your boss or other authority figures, ask yourself these questions:

- Whom does he or she remind me of?
- Whom or what do I act like when I am around him or her?
- Why do I give up so much of my own power to him or her?

The answers to these questions will help you to begin demystifying the boss-employee relationship. And finally, remember these wise words of Eleanor Roosevelt: "No one can make you feel inferior without your consent."

The Eight Secrets of Successfully Managing Up

Even in the most enlightened organizations, where the manager's title has been changed to team leader, coordinator, or something equally nonhierarchical, there still exist certain expectations for how followers should interact with leaders. Although on the surface there has been a shift toward the appearance of egalitarianism, the Golden Rule of Management still prevails: *He or she who has the gold sets the rules*. The degree to which you are able to work within the boundaries established by the boss, and to adapt to the changing expectations from one boss to another, largely determines your ultimate success in an organization.

Here are the eight secrets of successfully managing up:

1. **THE BOSS IS ONLY HUMAN, WITH STRENGTHS AND WEAKNESSES LIKE EVERYONE ELSE.** Expecting superhuman behavior from the boss, or thinking that you can aid in his or her development, is a little like trying to teach a pig to sing—it frustrates the teacher and annoys the pig. Reminding the boss about his or her weaknesses only serves to rub salt in the wound. Once you see the boss as human, you can overcome your childhood fantasies of having the perfect parent and interact with him or her on an adult-to-adult basis.

2. **THE BOSS WANTS YOU NOT ONLY TO DO YOUR JOB, BUT TO MAKE HIS OR HER JOB EASY AS WELL.** This is not to be confused with threatening the boss by acting as if you want his or her job. Every reasonable request that the boss makes should be met with the implicit or explicit response: *no problem*. On the other hand, if you foresee a problem, let the boss know in a way that encourages problem solving as opposed to presenting obstacles. Bosses don't want to hear that it can't be done; they want to know *how* it can be done. Seek opportunities to help the boss with his or her workload. Not only is it appreciated, but you get the chance to learn skills that will be helpful to your career.

3. **THE BOSS NEVER WANTS TO BE EMBARRASSED.** If you want to disagree with the boss, do it in private—even if it means calling a time-out during a meeting. If he or she decides to make

a correction to course given your input, it must ultimately be his or her decision. If a project fails or loses momentum due to the failure to heed your warning, in no way indicate, "I told you so." Continue to provide relevant information that will help to guide the project back on course.

4. **THE BOSS DOESN'T WANT TO HAVE TO TELL YOU WHAT TO DO.** But he or she wants to know what you're doing. You add value by thinking strategically, foreseeing what has to be done, and preempting the boss from having to give you continual instructions. By planning for upcoming events, projects, or special needs, you show that you are capable of more than simply the day-to-day activities. Avoid being a loose cannon, however, by informing your boss of what you're planning and asking for his or her input into the direction (no matter how much more technically capable you think you may be).

5. **THE BOSS, WHETHER OR NOT HE OR SHE ADMITS IT, WANTS YOU TO MAKE HIM OR HER LOOK GOOD.** In the long term, making him or her look good makes you look good. Rather than always looking for ways to showcase your accomplishments, find opportunities to make the team and your team leader look good. By so doing you will ultimately look like someone who is politically astute and capable of ultimately leading a team yourself.

6. **THE BOSS WANTS TO BE ABLE TO GIVE YOU FEEDBACK EASILY.** When given feedback, listen to it, ask for clarification if necessary, think about it, but don't argue with it. No one particularly likes giving feedback in the first place. Don't make it any tougher by arguing your point or trying to negate it in some way. Regardless of the veracity of the feedback, openly listening to it at least gives the impression that you're flexible and open to change. That's half the battle. The other half is making enough changes to meet the boss's expectations without feeling like you are compromising your own principles.

7. **THE BOSS, IN MOST CASES, IS NOT CAPABLE OF HELP-ING YOU WITH YOUR PERSONAL PROBLEMS.** Even the most patient, enlightened, and understanding bosses have trouble with bringing personal issues to the workplace. They may be genuinely empathetic, but the bottom line is that they don't want to play amateur psychologist—nor should you expect them to. The best bosses make special allowances now and then, but, as a rule, you shouldn't dwell on personal problems unless they are so severe that you know that they will seriously affect your performance. Doing otherwise sets you up for close scrutiny and eventual feedback related to the problem.

8. **THE BOSS WANTS YOU TO DELIVER WHAT YOU PROMISE.** The easiest way to destroy credibility is to renege on your promises—especially those made to the boss. If trust is built on consistency, then lack of trust stems from broken promises. Use the fifty-fifty rule for planning your workload: once you are given an assignment, you have half the amount of time until the deadline to ask questions and the other half to actually complete the project. If the boss doesn't hear from you within the first half of the time allotted for project completion, he or she assumes it will be done on time.

Managing Up with a Difficult Boss

The process of managing up is difficult enough when you have a rational, mature boss. It is nearly impossible when you have one who isn't. Most of us have had the challenge of working with a boss who thinks employees never do anything right. This may be because he or she didn't give sufficient information, constantly changed his or her mind about how things should be done, or was so disorganized that the rules constantly changed when new information came to the forefront. Whatever the reason, and there are as many reasons as there are difficult bosses, it is still your responsibility to manage up effectively. Regardless of the difficulty, he or she who has the gold *still* sets the rules.

One problem inherent with difficult bosses is that they can significantly diminish your confidence and self-esteem. This is yet another situation where early childhood experiences come into play. If a difficult boss reminds you of one of your parents or some other early authority figure, the likelihood that you will remain with him or her and be demoralized by his or her inappropriate behavior is greater than if this was not your experience. Ray is a good case in point.

A very talented graphic artist working in the animated films industry, Ray consistently produces high-quality results that are admired and valued by his clients. His boss (the company's owner), however, comes from the Neanderthal school of management. Despite the fact that Ray puts in seventy to eighty hours of work a week (with no additional compensation, since he is a "salaried" employee), he is never given a word of positive reinforcement by his boss. "My boss won't say anything that will make me feel good," says Ray. "It's as if he thinks it will go to my head and I'll ask for a raise. He doesn't want me to have any sense of control. What he doesn't understand is that a compliment now and then would actually make me work even harder and I wouldn't want any more money."

Ray could go anywhere else and write his own ticket. He's *that* talented. His problem is that his boss is exactly like his father—who never gave him a word of encouragement and kept tight control over Ray during his childhood. When others point out to Ray that he really should be looking elsewhere for a job, he comes up with a litany of excuses. Ray is bound by his history to repeat a familiar situation because it is in some ways comfortable. To leave would be symbolically to break the tie with his father.

If Ray's boss were not the company owner, the situation might be different. The difficulties that such bosses present to their followers typically do not go unnoticed by their superiors. One of two things happens: They derail because of the behavior, or they are kept in their positions because they do get the job done—even if it's at the expense of others. In their monograph, *Coping with an Intolerable Boss,* authors Michael Lombardo and Morgan McCall report their findings of interviews with seventy-three managers who were asked to tell about their experiences working with intolerable bosses. Lombardo and McCall found that patience and waiting the boss out is often the best course of action. Creating an adversarial situation only yields counterproductive results. Here's what they say:

> *Even an intolerable boss is still the boss. . . . A few of the managers [in the study] tried to change the boss, but in only six situations did a manager report any significant change in his superior's behavior as a result of the subordinate's efforts. The far more productive strategies were to change one's own response or, as a last resort, to get out of the situation.*

In the meantime, the question remains, how do you maintain your sanity and self-respect when working for an intolerable boss? Here are a few ideas for how you can maintain some semblance of control over your life in the face of a difficult situation:

• **See the boss as the boss—not as your mother or father.** As it should now be abundantly clear, you must first understand the effect that childhood experiences have on dealing with authority, then separate in your mind your boss from your parents or other authority figures. This is especially true when it comes to dealing with a difficult boss. He or she may unintentionally be pushing the same buttons that Mom or Dad did and you, therefore, react the same way as you did when you were a powerless child. When you find yourself angry or frustrated with the boss, first ask yourself whether you feel as you did when you were a child or as you feel around your parents. If so, switch gears and tell yourself that you are now an adult and give yourself permission to respond differently. Such a response may include the realization that you are not bonded by blood to this person and you can leave if you so choose.

• *Anticipate and prepare for difficult behavior.* Difficult bosses often exhibit the same behaviors over and over. If you take the time to analyze it, you can predict certain behaviors with quite a bit of accuracy. I once had a boss who, no matter how much time and effort I put into a report, would march into my office and pick it apart. It always made me feel guilty, as if I hadn't done enough work on it to begin with. In order to deal with him and my feelings about his response to my efforts, I made a game of keeping a tally of the number of things he claimed that I overlooked. I kept my little tally sheet underneath the phone in my office and whenever he left I added chit marks to the score. Anticipating his response, and making light of it without ignoring his comments, enabled me to maintain my self-confidence in the face of ongoing criticism.

• *Weigh the risks versus the benefits of telling the boss what you need.* Consider the possibility that the boss just doesn't have a clue about what he or she is doing that is creating a problem for you. Decide what could be the worst thing that would happen if you told him or her how you felt and what you needed in order to be more effective in your position. This must, of course, be done without affixing blame, but rather by giving an "I message." For example, if the boss consistently fails to give you enough information to do a project properly, you could say something like "I think I could be more effective if I had more details at the beginning of a project. Would it be possible to go over the specific requirements and how it fits into the bigger picture?" A riskier, but potentially even more beneficial, strategy would be to give the boss direct feedback as to how his or her behavior is affecting you. Still using the "I message" technique, you could say something like "I find it difficult to complete assignments efficiently because of the lack of information I'm given at the start of a project. I'm wondering whether it would be possible for you to be more specific when I begin rather than complete a project." If it doesn't work, you're no worse off than you were before having the conversation.

• *Remember that the best defense is a good offense.* This doesn't mean that you should be defensive with a difficult boss, even though it's easy to fall into that trap. Instead, it means that knowing what his or her hot buttons are, you should be thoroughly prepared and well organized in those particular areas. If the boss is a stickler for having a document free of typos, make certain that that's what you provide, even if it means having a colleague, or several colleagues, proofread your work for you. If it is tardiness that drives him or her up the wall, then you should be making herculean efforts to meet deadlines and arrive to work and meetings on time. For whatever reason, what may seem like a small thing to you is a big thing to the boss. Recognize what these things are, and head him or her off at the pass.

• *Evaluate the cost of staying in your position.* There comes the time when working with a difficult boss that you must ask yourself if it's worth it to stay. If in fact you have tried all of the things suggested above and the situation gets no better, you have only three alternatives: (1) put up with it hoping that the situation will change, (2) request a transfer within the company, or (3) quit. I have heard people say that they have to stay in their position because it pays well or because good jobs are hard to find, both of which are true, but there is a psychological cost to doing so. If the benefits of the job outweigh the cost in terms of damage to your self-confidence or self-esteem, then the logical choice is to stay and hope that the situation will eventually change. I have seen people wait it out and the boss eventually quits, is fired, or is promoted to another position. However, when the cost becomes too great, you have no alternative but to request a transfer (if the company is large enough) or to seek other employment. Most people with a difficult boss find that life improves significantly once the decision is made to leave, and once they actually begin a new job they wish they had done it sooner.

The ability to manage up is simply another element that successful people include in their skill sets. They know that good followership is as important as good leadership, and they make it easy for others to lead them. However, making it easy for others to lead can be difficult if the parameters of the employee-boss relationship are not clearly understood. Be realistic about the boss's expectations as well as how and to what extent they can be met. Most important, disengage from past personal circumstances and behaviors so that they don't obscure current workplace roles and relationships.

Ways to Manage Up

1. Always remember the Golden Rule of Management: He or she who has the gold sets the rules.
2. Choose your battles carefully—not every issue needs to be a battle, and you may win the battle but lose the war.
3. Make giving feedback to you easy by asking the boss how you can improve.
4. Never confront the boss in the presence of a higher authority.
5. Never make the boss look stupid or inept (even if he or she is).

6. Deliver more than what you're asked for.

7. Make yourself look good by making the boss look good.

8. Critically assess what you are asked to do, and make suggestions for improving on the original idea.

9. Lower your antennae for tuning into feelings that may belong more in childhood than in the present.

10. Use positive self-talk when feelings from the past do arise.

11. If the boss's position interferes with your confidence, pay more attention to the task than to the relationship.

12. Separate your image of the boss from that of your mother or father.

13. Weigh the risk versus the profit of giving the boss feedback.

14. View differences with the boss as just that— differences to be discussed and not confrontations to be won or lost.

15. Read the monograph *Coping with an Intolerable Boss* (see page 246).

16. Remember that you control no one's behavior except your own.

17. Have outside interests that capture your passion so that work issues can be put into perspective.

18. Be willing to give the boss your honest opinion and make every effort to influence him or her toward a decision that is in the best interest of the organization, but remember that the decision ultimately may not be yours.

19. Once a decision is made, fully support it—even if you disagree with it.

20. Keep your boss informed about what you are planning to do and ask for input.

21. Focus on the content of the boss's message rather than on how it is delivered.

22. Add value to your department and company by thinking ahead and identifying issues that the boss may not have thought of.

23. If you are inclined to acquiesce to authority, take more risks with standing up for what you believe in.

24. Consider the possibility that you may be better off in a different position or company.

Too Broad or Too Narrow Vision

BALANCE DETAIL ORIENTATION WITH STRATEGIC THINKING

An article entitled "How to Integrate Work and Deepen Expertise" (*Harvard Business Review,* Sept–Oct 1994) details a scenario that occurred nearly a decade ago when Kodak's product development group introduced the concept of a single-use, disposable camera. They envisioned that it could potentially become a popular item with people who didn't own a camera or had forgotten their own. Since they viewed the project as something involving the use of high-tech film, executives gave the idea to their film development department and asked that they work on it. The staff of the film department, however, didn't share their colleagues' enthusiasm for the project. Believing that a disposable camera would only decrease sales of the already profitable film that Kodak sold, the department dragged its feet and paid little attention to its development.

We all know how the story ends. The disposable camera was developed and has become a highly successful addition to Kodak's product line. It was developed not by the film development department, but by Kodak's camera division, who saw the value of management's original vision for the product and acted on it. Whereas the film development staff looked narrowly at the potential of the product and allowed initial skepticism to interfere with development, the camera division looked broadly at the possibilities and developed a real winner for Kodak.

The story emphasizes the importance of balancing detail orientation with strategic thinking. Most of us seem to have a natural inclination to pay attention to either the nitty-gritty details or to the bigger picture. It is what makes us choose professions in, for example, accounting, medical technology, and administration over those in research, social work, or architecture. This is not to say that there aren't people in accounting who enjoy seeing the bigger picture or people who prefer a detail orientation in research, but rather that such preferences often influence our choice of career and our ultimate success in those professions.

If you will refer back to the MBTI® Preferences Chart (Reason #2, pages 72–73), you will notice that on the Attending scale (what a person likes to pay attention to) there are two types of people: sensers and intuitors. This gives us our greatest clue to whether we prefer details or the big picture. Whereas sensers prefer to deal with what is concrete, real, and tangible, intuitors are happier operating in the realm of theory and possibility. As you peruse the two lists, think about where you fit in. One source of job dissatisfaction can arise from being in a job that is counter to your natural inclination.

Another way of understanding these preferences comes from research pertaining to the brain's functioning. We know that the left and right hemispheres of the brain each process and handle information in distinctly different ways. Betty Edwards, in her work *Drawing on the Right Side of the Brain,* explains that the left hemisphere "analyzes, abstracts, counts, marks time, plans step-by-step procedures, verbalizes, [and] makes rational statements based on logic," whereas the right hemisphere helps us to "understand metaphors, dream, [and] create new combinations of ideas." Her contention, that our culture and educational system tend to focus on and value left hemisphere activity, explains why so many of us have difficulty bringing our more creative selves to the forefront. It isn't that we don't have creative capability, it is that the capability isn't developed and languishes from lack of use.

It is no wonder, then, that so many corporations suffer from a lack of creativity. The strengths that most of us have in right-brain functioning are not balanced with left-brain activity. Long after we lose our effectiveness, we continue to do the same things in the same way. We fail to draw on our capacity to envision our products or services differently and, instead, perpetuate the status quo. We maintain, but we don't create, thereby losing the competitive edge. This becomes especially problematic when the people who are entrusted to lead organizations are saddled only with strength in right brain functioning.

People who avoid premature derailment are good at both. They don't sacrifice close attention to detail for broader, more strategic thinking and vice versa. They successfully balance detail orientation with a view of the bigger picture. Use the following checklist to see how good you are at this balancing act.

_____ I am equally good at seeing the forest through the trees as the trees through the forest.

_____ Given a project, I first think about how it fits into the overall scheme of things and then become involved in the details of making it happen.

_____ I can take a good idea and turn it into a reality.

_____ I don't get bogged down in analysis paralysis.

_____ I find it as easy to come up with better ways of doing routine tasks as it is to develop processes for implementing these ideas.

_____ I'm patient with projects that require close attention to detail.

_____ I am seldom bored during brainstorming sessions.

_____ If I had the technical ability to do both, it would be as appealing to me to design a house as it would be to actually build it.

_____ I balance my checkbook regularly, but I don't spend an inordinate amount of time trying to find where it may be off by a few cents.

_____ It is fairly easy for me to see and hear nuances in messages and interpersonal communication.

Strategic Thinking + Attention to Detail = Success

Thomas Alva Edison, possibly the most prolific inventor of the nineteenth century, is an example of a historical figure who successfully balanced attention to detail with strategic thinking. Never a particularly good student, Edison was described as "addled" by one teacher, and another teacher described his classroom behavior as "dreamy, inattentive, with a tendency to drift off during recitations." These comments motivated Edison's mother to take him out of public school and tutor him herself. Even as a child, Edison exhibited the essence of a true visionary: curiosity. In adulthood, that same curiosity and willingness to take risks made him one of the most successful inventors of our time. By the age of twenty-one Edison had invented a stock ticker-tape machine, and throughout his life he produced more than one thousand invaluable devices, such as the electric light bulb, steam-driven power stations, the alkaline storage battery, celluloid film, the movie projector, and the phonograph, the invention in which he took the most pride. Edison had vision, but he also had the technical competence and proficiency to make those visions a reality.

On the business front, Elizabeth Claiborne (better known as Liz) provides an inspirational example of someone who had a vision and developed a strategy to turn it into a billion-dollar Fortune 500 company. With a background in art, she worked her way up the ladder of fashion design, ultimately becoming chief designer for Jonathan Logan. Despite her frustration over the fact that she could not sell her fashion vision to her employer, she remained with the company for sixteen years. Like many career women, she deferred her own dream while her husband pursued his and until her children were safely through college. Finally, in 1975, at age forty-six, Claiborne invested her family's life savings ($50,000) to form the fashion giant that shares her name.

Claiborne intuitively knew what fashions should be designed and marketed to working women and at what price. When she started her business this was a largely untapped market. Her less visionary colleagues continued producing clothes designed for pencil-thin models, not the average female figure, while Claiborne saw and filled a gap in the clothes market. Her strategy was to design mix-and-match clothes, decide how much women would be willing to pay for each design, and then negotiate to have them produced in Asia at a cost consistent with the sales price.

Within six years of starting the business, Liz Claiborne clothing generated $117 million in revenues and soon thereafter went public. Within ten years Claiborne's personal net worth was estimated to be $200 million. Within fifteen years of operation sales were double those of her established competitors and the company was named the Fortune 500's most profitable firm. Today, the company dominates the field of women's better sportswear with a 33 percent market share, generating more than $2 billion annually in revenues.

Edison and Claiborne are quite different examples, but similar in that they are two ordinary human beings who produced ex-

The Detail/Strategic Thinking Continuum

ACUTE ATTENTION TO DETAIL	BALANCED ATTENTION TO DETAIL AND STRATEGIC THINKING	OVERUTILIZED STRATEGIC THINKING
Acute attention is paid to minute detail and to doing the job in a prescribed, routine way, while outside factors that affect the work are neglected, overlooked, or seen as impediments to task accomplishment. Project completion may suffer due to overconcern with detail.	A project is looked at in its entirety with all variables being considered, including the human resources that are required, innovations that would make it more valuable, and a specific plan for carrying it out in the most efficient and cost-effective manner.	Ideas and concepts are of prime importance, while practical implications for executing ideas are overlooked. Projects are stalled due to ongoing changes, revisions, and analyses.

traordinary results. Countless great ideas never become reality because people can't attend to the details required to carry them through. An idea without a plan for executing it is only a dream. Close adherence to detail conceptualization maintains status quo. The ability to think broadly and act intentionally forms the core of balancing detail orientation with strategic thinking.

With a little practice, we are each capable of functioning on the dual levels of detail orientation and strategic thinking. There is a continuum that goes from highly detail-oriented to overly concerned with the big picture (see chart above).

As you move toward the center of the continuum there is an increased balance between the two extremes that provides for maximum job effectiveness. People at either extreme are limited in the value that they add to a job or project. Ideally, we would surround ourselves in the work environment with people who complement our strengths, but because this is typically not possible, the job is either done routinely, with little concern for innovation or customer needs, or is stalled entirely due to analysis paralysis.

Jim Harkins, director of business and strategic planning at AlliedSignal Aerospace, introduced me to the concept of *strategic intent,* which is another way to approach strategic thinking. He cites numerous examples of companies that had broad visions for what they wanted to accomplish and developed specific plans for how to achieve them—in spite of seemingly insurmountable odds. One case in point is Canon Business Machines, Inc., in Costa Mesa, California. Canon's management made the strategic decision to not take on the leader in the field, Xerox, but instead to develop inexpensive copiers and provide services ancillary to their use. With this *strategic intent,* Canon has become better than any of its competitors at building the copier's printing engine and in the process earned the respect of customers and colleagues.

Major corporations such as IBM, GM, and Sears nearly self-destructed in the 1980s because of their failure to do what Canon did—redefine their visions of the future. They were so caught up in their routines, and what worked yesterday, that they neglected to see the changes in customer needs and what was needed to be successful tomorrow. Strategic intent works for companies and for individuals who want to avoid derailment. Attention to the future helps you to focus on what's important, guide your career, and make value-added contributions to your organization.

The business world is full of individuals who have derailed due to the inability to balance detail orientation and strategic thinking.

In his presentations to corporate leaders, Harvard professor John Kotter routinely mentions that the airline industry provides us with two such examples of high-profile personalities: Frank Borman, formerly president of Eastern Airlines, and Donald Burr, founder of the once wildly popular airline People Express. Clearly, both men achieved great things in their careers, but both men also prematurely derailed due to overreliance on their unique strengths.

Most of us remember Frank Borman as the commander of the first human flight around the moon. He went on to become president of Eastern Airlines in 1975, a position he held until he resigned in 1986 under less than favorable conditions. As a child, he spent hours engrossed in building model airplanes—a somewhat solitary activity. His schoolmates didn't want much to do with him because they found him to be so bossy—which left him even more isolated. Borman went on to attend West Point. He is remembered there as someone who was staunchly independent. When an upperclassman intentionally stamped on his foot as part of the traditional hazing process (where underclassmen are expected to grin and bear it), Borman instead "called him a son of a bitch and threatened to kill him." When he graduated in 1950, his training as a pilot combined with a scientific education enabled him to become an astronaut in the Gemini program.

Not surprisingly, given his character and background, Borman earned the reputation at Eastern as a *command and control* leader. His goal for the struggling airline was to "restore discipline and profitability." The only problem was that he wanted to accomplish this while at the same time treating his staff like functionaries. He expected them to respond in much the same way as an aircraft would to his deft maneuvering: swiftly and unquestioningly. Borman never understood that his success depended on looking at the bigger picture, seeing how people fit into strategies, and how creative problem solving would be his only salvation—not command and control. He pounded employees with letters about the problems Eastern was facing and underscored his expectation that everyone would sacrifice for the good of the whole. His training as an engineer precluded him from balancing a strong orientation toward controlling detail with creatively and strategically seeking solutions to his company's problems.

Donald Burr, on the other hand, suffered from the opposite limited skill set. From childhood he approached everything he did with passion. As a youth he was even a proselytizer for his church, traveling from city to city to recruit other teens into a fellowship program. He approached his work in much the same way. Aviation was more than just a career to him—it was a "romance." In 1981 Burr started his own airline, People Express, after walking out on former boss Frank Lorenzo at Texas International Airlines. He had a vision for a "no frills" airline where passengers benefited from low prices and friendly service and employees from an exciting and rewarding work environment. He made it a contingency of employment that all employees own stock in the company. Burr himself conducted much of new-employee training, using his proselytizing skill to generate enthusiasm and rally people behind his vision.

At the time, the concept of cheap fares was a radical one: other airlines would charge $189 to $250 or more for the same flight that would cost only $79 on People Express. In order to do this, Burr shifted outside the normal airline paradigm and expanded the scope of each job, limited services offered, and made employees partners in the business. Whereas Eastern had dozens of job categories and a terrible relationship with its unions, People Express had only three categories: the people who fly the plane, the people who fix the plane, and everyone else. A truly creative solution to rising airfares. So why did Burr derail? Because he failed to manage the details inherent to his business and listen to his advisers who tried to talk him out of expanding when there were no systems in place to manage the expansion. His staff, including top management, burned out while Burr continued hammering away at the vision. Burr was great when it came to developing a vision, but short on attention to the kinds of details that ultimately derailed him.

You may be surprised when you read that a person who has successfully combined the two skill sets is a woman who works with cosmetics and has a penchant for pink Cadillacs—Mary Kay Ash, founder of Mary Kay Cosmetics. She began her business with a clear strategic intent: to create a company that would enable women to be financially independent while permitting them to focus on God first, family second, and work third. Next, she had the foresight to surround herself with good people who complemented her own natural abilities. Mary Kay thought strategically and planned thoughtfully—and to this day that combination of skills contributes significantly to her success and the success of everyone involved with Mary Kay Cosmetics. When less enlightened leaders attempt to embarrass her about the fact that she rewards employees with pink Cadillacs, her typical response is, "What color Cadillacs do you give to *your* employees?"

Square Pegs in Round Holes

People with a natural inclination for either detail orientation or strategic thinking often choose jobs that enable them to rely on one or the other skill. It is not coincidence that those who are happy working for the IRS generally have an ability to pay acute attention to detail, whereas those who find job satisfaction at NASA or the Jet Propulsion Laboratory are likely to be strategic thinkers. Both types of people, however, may find themselves in a quandary when they are forced into a job or assignment that requires the complementary behavior. Just one skill or the other isn't enough to assure continued success.

A few years ago, a client of mine had a significant reduction in its workforce, entirely eliminating its public relations department. One staff member, whom I will call Amanda, had been with the company for nearly twenty years and her management wanted to reward her loyalty by finding a place for her in another department. Amanda had been a public relations coordinator and, as such, had significant contact with the media, senior executives, and esteemed guests. She was superb at finessing all of the relationships involved in her job.

Amanda's management was pleased when they found her a job as a clerk in their benefits department. Now they wouldn't have to lay her off. Amanda herself was pleased as well—at least in the beginning. After Amanda had been in the new job for several months, I called her to see how she was doing. This normally upbeat and optimistic woman was extremely unhappy in her new job and was thinking about leaving the company. When I probed into what the problem was, she said that she couldn't stand working alone day after day and paying such close attention to the most minute details that her job required.

For twenty years Amanda was used to seeing the big picture, juggling multiple tasks and people, and paying close attention to people problems. When she was put into a job that required close attention to detail and afforded little contact with people, it wasn't so much that she *couldn't* do it, but that she didn't *want* to do it. And herein lies the mistake that so many companies make: when people fail to succeed in their positions, they send them for training rather than assess their suitability for the job. The fact is, most of us can do whatever we put our minds to provided, of course, that we have the necessary basic skills. When we're not doing what we are capable of, it does no good to get more training. Job satisfaction comes from doing what we're good at and what we have a natural inclination toward. When we enjoy our work, we are more likely to be able to balance the big picture with the details required to do it.

A case in point is that of a woman who was sent for coaching because she "wasn't detail oriented enough and displayed poor judgment." When her boss was asked to be more specific, he gave the example of how she chose the wrong kind of furniture for the executive offices. Instead of choosing conservative, dark wood, she chose to go with a lighter, more contemporary look. Before my first meeting with the woman, I went to the executive floor to take a look at the furniture. It was a lovely choice that complemented the surroundings, but it couldn't be called conservative.

At our first meeting, I asked the woman why she thought coaching had been suggested for her. She said that she supposed it was because she didn't fit in. She had an artistic background and she had been hired as an interior decorator for the company based on her knowledge of design. Nevertheless, her management always second-guessed her decisions. She brought to our second meeting a portfolio of watercolor paintings that were incredibly beautiful. As she proudly displayed each one, she said that this was what she wanted to be doing—painting. It occurred to me as I looked at the paintings that one has to have an eye for detail in order to be able to paint on the scale of which she was clearly capable. On the other hand, she had to see the world in a way that was very different from that of her corporate counterparts. It wasn't that she didn't have detail orientation or that she lacked good judgment, she simply wasn't inclined to pay attention to the details required in her job.

Both this woman and Amanda were fortunate to have enough self-confidence not to settle for jobs for which they were ill suited. Once Amanda recognized the true nature of her problem, she asked for a transfer to a different type of work that would more fully use her talents. She's now working happily as the administrative assistant in a busy department where she gets to interact with many different types of people and use her fine administrative skills. And as for the artist—she's now living in Taos, New Mexico, a perfect setting for artists and watercolor painting.

Just because you aren't detail or big-picture oriented in one situation, doesn't mean you can't be in another. The trick is to find work that allows you to use both skills and to know when to apply each. The more you like your work, the greater the likelihood that you'll be able to call on the full range of your capabilities instead of relying exclusively on just a few strengths. It is the balance that assures success and enables you to avoid derailment.

One last anecdote before providing you with some suggestions for how to find that balance. I received a call from a man whom I had met during a supervisory-skills training program. He said that he was going to do an employee's annual performance review and wanted to run by me what he was going to say to make sure he wasn't being too subjective. He faxed me the review, and as I was studying it I noticed that it pretty much revolved around the need to develop more follow-through and attention to detail. When I called him back to discuss it, I mentioned that it seemed as though the employee might not enjoy what he was doing. Generally, when people like their work, they quite naturally pay attention to the details of it and complete it in a timely fashion. In other words, we do well the things we like doing and put off doing things we don't enjoy. After a moment's pause, the man said that was indeed true. He had spoken on numerous occasions with the employee about the fact that he seemed mismatched for the job, but that there were no more suitable jobs available in the company at the time.

I don't envy the manager who has to coach someone who is doing work that he or she dislikes. When an employee tries to fit into the wrong job, his or her energy is diverted by trying to make the work fit, rather than doing the job efficiently and effectively. Your ultimate success depends on doing work that you love and for which you are well suited. You cannot expect to achieve peak performance when you are not interested in the fundamental nature of your work. Certainly, there are aspects of all jobs that we may not like but need to do nonetheless. We have to learn to do these tasks with enthusiasm and attention equal to that which we bring to the tasks that we enjoy. Satisfaction comes from the nature of the work and our enjoyment of it. Balancing details and the big picture is much easier when you are in the right job than it is when you're doing something simply because it pays well or because someone always expected you would do it.

Factors Contributing to a Narrow Focus

The tendency to focus on details to the exclusion of the bigger picture is characterized by the need to micromanage people and processes, overattendance to minutiae, and the inability to see the relationships between issues or factors. People with high detail orientation typically do well in jobs that require precision and meticulous singular concentration. It is a wonderful gift to be precise and focus on detail, but it can be a derailment factor if not balanced with the opposite—the ability to think strategically.

Although there is evidence that the inclinations toward either detail orientation or strategic thinking are something we are born with, both can become overdeveloped. For example, logical, linear thinking, or detail orientation, is valued in our educational system. Overdevelopment of this particular strength can also stem from the need to function effectively in a chaotic childhood home or from having parents who were not sufficiently attentive to the child's needs. The child, then, learns to compensate for this household deficit by becoming hypervigilant. Fearing that important things will be overlooked or neglected entirely, he or she assures nothing is missed by paying close attention to the details of daily life. Paradoxically, however, things *are* overlooked because he or she is not able to view the entire situation.

In the workplace, acute attention to detail is displayed by people who follow instructions religiously and honor tried-and-true ways of doing things. They may be given an assignment with incorrect instructions and, instead of realizing that the instructions are wrong, they continue along the path until someone else points out the error of their ways. For example, when told to "hold all calls and take messages," a person may do as instructed, but fail to realize that when the company president calls it might be appropriate to put that particular call through (or at least check to see whether the boss wants to take the call). Or, someone may prepare reports with illogical conclusions because they fail to see that there has been a mistake in a formula or procedure used to reach those conclusions. This is why outstanding bookkeepers may not make particularly good financial analysts. The skills required to be accurate are not the same ones required to assess the broader financial picture. It is easy to see how someone with strong detail orientation adds only limited value to an organization.

In addition to the childhood factors contributing to detail orientation, there are a number of other reasons why people fail to think strategically. They include:

• **FEAR.** A significant factor contributing to the inability to see the bigger picture is fear. In an effort to get it "right," some people miss the nuances in a message. They try too hard and wind up listening selectively. The fear may be generalized and apply to all situations or only to those that involve people in authority. I recall early in my career giving instructions to an assistant to cancel the arrangements previously made for a visit to a particular city. She asked me for all of the details about the date, flight, and airline and then canceled these, but neglected to cancel all concomitant plans such as car, hotel, etc. She was great when given specific instructions, but she could not take the next step to assure that all related aspects of a project were similarly attended to. The woman's fear of making a mistake caused her to miss the bigger picture in favor of focusing on a specific task. The value that she could add was limited by this fear.

• **RIGIDITY.** People who engage in ritualistic or other narrowly defined behavior frequently can't see new and different ways of doing things. They plod along the same path, every day, in the same way. They would never think of driving a different way to work, eating something different for breakfast, or solving a problem in an unorthodox way. Instead, they do things in prescribed and familiar ways. When asked why they didn't do something in a more effective way, they often reply that it never occurred to them. Rigidity impedes the ability to think broadly and strategically.

• **THE INABILITY TO DEAL WITH AMBIGUITY.** I've never forgotten a line from a college textbook that said something to the effect, "The sign of the mentally healthy person is the one who can deal best with ambiguity because that's all life is—ambiguous." Those people who must deal with the known, as opposed to the possible, have tremendous difficulty thinking broadly. By operating within a constant comfort zone of what is known, as opposed to what could be, such people never take the kinds of risks required to successfully balance detail orientation with strategic thinking.

• **HIGH SENSE OF URGENCY.** If there is a high sense of urgency, individuals may focus so hard on completing the task that they miss the how, why, and what of the project. In an effort to get the job done expediently, they fail to see how it may tie in to the bigger picture. Ironically, the opposite end of the spectrum— being too involved in the big picture to the exclusion of attention to detail—can also result from a high sense of urgency for reasons that will be discussed later.

- **LOW SENSE OF URGENCY.** This factor affects people on both ends of the spectrum as well. People with an overdeveloped detail orientation and a low sense of urgency frequently underestimate the amount of time they actually have to complete a project and spend an inordinate amount of time on the technicalities involved. They spend their time making fail-safe plans, nitpicking, and reviewing the most mundane details as opposed to understanding that a project must be completed both accurately and in a timely fashion.

- **NARROWLY DEFINED ROLES.** One mistake made by many businesses is to define employee roles too narrowly. This was a trend in the 1970s and 1980s, and a generation of "specialists" emerged. People were asked to do one thing really well. They developed a depth of knowledge in their fields but lacked a breadth of experience that would later be useful to them. When the layoffs of the 1990s hit, they were ill equipped to take on broader responsibilities. Although job descriptions provide an in-depth understanding of a particular role, they can narrow the employee's perspective and expectations. In the past, organizations had plenty of people with each type of preference—detail and big-picture people—to meet their needs. As they have downsized, however, it is expected that the people remaining will be able to function comfortably in both arenas. It is now more critical than ever that people be able to both initiate and implement new ideas—a feat requiring both detail and strategic thinking skills.

Ways to Develop Strategic Thinking

The shift from detail orientation to strategic thinking is probably the toughest behavioral change suggested in this book. It requires not only specific behavioral changes, but also changes in how you look at the world. The factors contributing to the former are so strong that they completely eclipse the ability to engage in the latter. Even the term *strategic thinking* is ominous to some who perceive this function to be the exclusive domain of people in think tanks or strategic planning jobs. Instead, it is simply a way of describing the behaviors required to think more broadly.

The following suggestions can help you become a strategic thinker:

1. **AVOID TAKING NOTES WHEN SOMEONE IS TALKING TO YOU.** The technique of active listening described under Reason #1 works well here. In order to comprehend the entire picture, you can't grasp only one aspect of it. I once coached a woman who tried to write down everything I said (can you guess what she had to work on?). Inevitably, she missed the point of what I was saying by attempting to capture the details. Surrender yourself to the speaker, ask questions, and paraphrase what you've just heard. This will allow you to hear and understand the subtleties of the message.

2. **ASK YOURSELF, "WHAT IS THE BIGGER PICTURE HERE?"** Take time from the task to think momentarily about what it means, how it fits into other projects, and why you are being asked to do it. Avoid the tendency to jump into a project before you've thought it through completely. Learn to become comfortable with negligible delays—especially when those delays are for the purpose of up-front planning. Most assignments aren't as urgent as you might initially think. You may even be imposing your own sense of urgency where there is none.

3. **CONSCIOUSLY SEEK WAYS TO IMPROVE PROCESSES.** Instead of doing the job in the same old way, think about how you might do it more efficiently or creatively. If necessary, get input from others about how they might approach the same task. Make suggestions for improving processes in ways that might prove to

be more cost-effective or in some other way add value to your department or company.

4. **READ BOOKS AND JOURNAL ARTICLES THAT EXPAND YOUR UNDERSTANDING OF TRENDS IN YOUR FIELD OF EXPERTISE.** All too often we read only materials that address the technical aspects of how we do our jobs. This is important, but equally important are materials that ask you to think about where your field is headed, current challenges that it faces, and concepts that go beyond business as usual. See yourself as someone who anticipates and responds to the requirements of the future, not just reacts to it.

5. **BROADLY DEFINE YOUR ROLE.** Whether you are a secretary, first-line supervisor, or division vice president, look for ways in which your role interfaces with those of coworkers, other departments and companies, or customers. Talk to these people about their needs and ways in which you can partner with them in an effort to add value, and envision yourself at the center of a complex network rather than as a lone performer. Consider the possibility that you can create the ideal job for yourself by expanding, not changing, your role.

6. **RESIST PERFECTIONISM.** Perfectionists spend so much time attending to details that they often fail to see the large issues involved in a project. They wind up missing the clues to success that often lie in the periphery. Rather than spend time perfecting perfection, use that time to think broadly and strategically about critical points of interface, better ways to do the job, and anticipate tomorrow's trends.

7. **BE CREATIVE.** Betty Edwards's *Drawing on the Right Side of the Brain* and Julia Cameron's *The Artist's Way* are places to start. Both books provide exercises that stimulate right-brain thinking. You can also take classes in creative writing, drawing, or acting that will help you express your innate, creative talents. Most im-

portant, don't worry about being good at it or doing it right; do it for fun.

How Overutilization of Strategic Thinking Can Cause Derailment

Any strength taken to the extreme becomes your greatest liability. Even if you work in the most creative of environments where possibilities abound, such as a movie studio, fashion design house, or genetics engineering laboratory, you are still expected to produce well-thought-out and practical results. People who are gifted with the ability to think broadly, creatively, or strategically often suffer from analysis paralysis. They become so caught up in the idea that they overlook the need to turn the idea into reality.

I once worked with a man who was brilliant at conceptualization. He could come up with ideas for any major project on which our company was working. If you wanted to brainstorm, he was the man to go to. The only problem was that he was short on implementation. He often provided solutions so complex that they couldn't possibly be carried out cost-effectively. He was unable to work within boundaries and was forever exceeding his budget without really producing results. When the company went through a downsizing, he was one of the first people tapped because his contribution to the organization was limited. He couldn't make his dreams a reality.

Another form of overutilization of strategic thinking comes with people who are manic. They are often off the scale of the creative continuum. You may know some of these folks. They are energetic, enthusiastic, and innovative—but so much so that they exceed the bounds of acceptable behavior. They tire us mortals out with their continual flow of ideas and concepts. They are frequently successful in entrepreneurial efforts, provided they don't overextend their resources, because they believe in their ability to overcome any obstacle and won't take "no" for an answer. They are less successful in the corporate arena because they typically can't function within the bounds of expected social and group behavior and are perceived as loose cannons by their management.

The factors contributing to overutilization of strategic thinking are not quite as clear-cut as those contributing to acute attention to detail. Certain types of personalities seem more inclined to be able to think broadly and creatively than others. Certainly being raised in a home or working in an environment where creativity is valued and encouraged is a plus, but there must also be a degree of imagination in the individual to begin with. Whereas innovativeness can be thwarted and not allowed to blossom fully, the opposite is not always true. It may be more difficult for people who have never developed a creative pursuit to develop an ability to innovate later in their lives, no matter how much they are encouraged to do so. Yet we can all stretch the boundaries of thinking that confine us by rejecting strict adherence to outdated norms, self-limiting paradigms, and early childhood messages that have outlived their usefulness.

For those of you who think too broadly and strategically and overlook the importance of producing results, the following suggestions should help you achieve balance with greater attention to detail.

• *Schedule time for both project development and project implementation.* When you are given an assignment, allocate a specific amount of time to be used for brainstorming, research, or development. Resist the tendency to use more time than you have allocated or to cut short the implementation period. On the front end, realistically assess how much time it will actually take to complete the project once it is designed and schedule adequate time to meet that requirement. To avoid being top-heavy with creative types, be certain to include people who complement your strengths on project teams.

• *Solicit input from (and listen to) your more practical colleagues.* Bounce your ideas off people you can trust who can see the realities of a situation. Ask them for their opinion of the practicality of your ideas, reasonableness of direction, and value to the company or customer. Rather than viewing these people as overly simplistic or obstacles to your brilliant ideas, consider the counterpoint that they offer as valuable insight into what the organization might expect or find feasible.

• *Consider your audience.* When making presentations, consider the fact that you will most likely have to influence an array of personality types, most of whom don't share your big-picture orientation. Couch your remarks within a framework that will stretch the imaginations of the most conservative people in the audience without making them roll their eyes in disbelief or think that you are from another planet. Remember to include well-thought-out suggestions for how your idea can be implemented practically and efficiently.

• *Find an outlet for external creative endeavors.* If you work in an organization that just doesn't appreciate your creativity or ability to think strategically, ensure that you have outlets in your personal life to exercise those talents. Join clubs, write books, paint pictures, or associate with like-minded people who will validate and encourage you. A very creative woman who worked down the hall from me had a boring, mundane job poring over tables, data runs, and figures all day long. But to her, her work wasn't her life. Her life started when she left at 5:00 P.M.

• *Consider the possibility that you are in the wrong job.* As with the artist who is now in Taos painting, it is an awful feeling to think that you have to sublimate your greatest gifts in order to fit into your organization. Once you've tried all of the things suggested above, and you still can't quite focus on detail and planning to the degree that your management wants you to, then you might do better switching to a job or career that will value and use your unique skill set. There is a caveat here, however: *Wherever you go, you bring you with you,* and that means that your developmental areas as well as your strengths follow you from job to job. Although a more creative environment may not expect such excessive attention to detail, they will most likely expect *some* attention to it. Changing jobs typically doesn't solve the problem entirely.

Although balance is required in all the suggestions for overcoming your strengths contained so far in this book, it is in the areas of detail orientation and strategic thinking that it is most critical. Good technical skills balance good people skills, but good technical skills don't balance excessive detail orientation or overutilized strategic thinking. They balance each other.

Developing Skill in Strategic Thinking

1. Take a stress-management class so that you don't succumb to the need to treat everything with the utmost urgency.
2. Develop the patience and foresight needed to think strategically by learning to play chess.
3. Take small risks by doing things differently from the way you usually do them.
4. Look for the relationships between things instead of focusing on one thing at a time.
5. Plan projects before beginning them so as to allot sufficient time for completion in a timely manner.

6. Subscribe to a magazine that addresses trends in your field of expertise.

7. Trust your ability to do things right the first time, and then use the remaining time to plan for the future.

8. Think about your role and your contribution to your organization broadly instead of limiting yourself to a job description or job title.

9. Question and stretch the rules now and then.

10. Spend time brainstorming a project with creative colleagues before diving into it.

11. Once a week, take a different route to work.

12. Take a class in drawing, writing, or sculpture just for fun to open your mind to the possibilities.

Developing Detail Orientation

13. Take a time-management class so that you can more effectively balance design and implementation time.

14. Consider the practicalities of implementation before suggesting solutions.

15. Strictly adhere to deadlines—missed deadlines should be the exception rather than the rule.

16. Meditate to help improve your focus.

17. Be certain that presentations include concern for conceptual validity and practical implementation.

18. Carefully prepare your message in your mind before you give your opinion.

19. Before beginning a project draw a schematic, flowchart, or other visual to help you focus on the practicalities.

20. Ask detail-oriented colleagues for input into the logistics of a project.

21. Volunteer to chair meetings and use an agenda to keep the group on track.

22. If you are a manager, hire staff who complement your own natural ability with their attention to detail.

23. Avoid taking on unnecessary or low priority projects before you've completed more critical ones.

24. Balance your checkbook.

Indifference to Customer or Client Needs

DEVELOP A "CAN-DO" ATTITUDE

I recently was waiting in the lobby of a large and well-known nonprofit agency when the receptionist answered the phone. Although I could only hear half the conversation, I got the gist of what must have been said on the other end based on her responses. It went something like this:

Caller: *Can you tell me where you're located?*
Receptionist: *6578 West Main.*
Caller: *What's the cross street?*
Receptionist: *Sixth Street.*
Caller: *What exit is that off of the freeway?*
Receptionist: *Belleview.*
Caller: *Are you east or west of the freeway?*
Receptionist: *West.*
Caller: *Are there any landmarks?*
Receptionist: *There's a hospital on the corner.*
Caller: *I'm familiar with that area, but I can't picture your building.*

Receptionist: *We're behind the hospital.*
Caller: *Thanks.*
Receptionist: [No response, just hangs up.]

Listening to the conversation, I was struck by the fact that the receptionist did nothing to help this person, who was obviously trying to figure out how to get to the building, find his or her way there. Despite the fact that the building is situated behind the hospital that she mentioned, and therefore easy to miss for a first-time visitor (I had the problem myself), she simply answered the questions she was asked.

The situation provides a good example of indifference to customer or client needs and the unwillingness to do anything more than minimally required. I am certain that if the receptionist were asked why she wasn't more helpful, she would be indignant at the implication. After all, she answered the questions the caller posed to her. How much different an impression the caller (and I) would have had if the conversation went something like this instead:

Caller: *Can you tell me where you're located?*
Receptionist: *Where are you coming from?*
Caller: *The north end of town.*
Receptionist: *You'll take the freeway south to the Belleview exit and turn left. Go about four stoplights to Sixth and turn right. When you reach Main, you'll see a hospital on the right corner. Go another half block and turn right into the first driveway. We're located directly behind the hospital.*
Caller: *Thanks.*
Receptionist: *My pleasure.*

Doing your job is no longer enough to ensure your success. People who avoid career derailment go above and beyond the obvious job requirements or requests—they anticipate needs and meet them without being prodded. Many of the behaviors discussed in the previous chapters contribute to what is commonly called a can-do attitude. For example, people who have relationships in place that contribute to getting the job done, who see the bigger picture and not only the details involved in a project, and who manage up successfully are more likely to view new or potentially complex assignments as interesting challenges rather than as obstacles to getting their routine tasks out of the way. Such people have the tools required to react confidently to nearly any request that may come their way.

A can-do attitude is exemplified by the second scenario described above as opposed to the first. It is having the outlook that "I'm not sure *how* I'll do it, but it *will* get done," as opposed to something more ambivalent like "I'm not sure I can do that," or even worse, a response that shuts the door entirely, such as "That's just not possible." Another way of looking at a can-do attitude is having a customer-service orientation, recognizing that *all those people with whom you interact are, in fact, your customers.*

People with a can-do attitude tend to check off most of the items on this list:

     _____ I look at barriers to goal achievement as challenges, not insurmountable obstacles.

     _____ I tend to be overly optimistic about how much I can accomplish in a day.

     _____ It is unusual for me to turn down uncommon or special requests.

     _____ I view my colleagues, management, and clients as my customers.

     _____ I gain a great deal of personal satisfaction from knowing that I went the extra mile for someone.

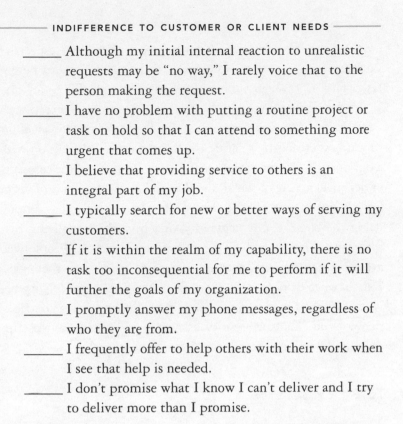

_____ Although my initial internal reaction to unrealistic requests may be "no way," I rarely voice that to the person making the request.

_____ I have no problem with putting a routine project or task on hold so that I can attend to something more urgent that comes up.

_____ I believe that providing service to others is an integral part of my job.

_____ I typically search for new or better ways of serving my customers.

_____ If it is within the realm of my capability, there is no task too inconsequential for me to perform if it will further the goals of my organization.

_____ I promptly answer my phone messages, regardless of who they are from.

_____ I frequently offer to help others with their work when I see that help is needed.

_____ I don't promise what I know I can't deliver and I try to deliver more than I promise.

A can-do attitude is typified by the willingness and desire to serve the customer, meet all reasonable requests, go above and beyond the call of duty, and find creative ways to solve seemingly insurmountable problems. It is the opposite of what psychologist and author Dr. Judith Bardwick calls an attitude of _entitlement_. In her book _Danger in the Comfort Zone,_ Bardwick describes the phenomenon of entitlement as "an attitude, a way of looking at life. Those who have this attitude believe that they do not have to earn what they get. They come to believe that they get something because they are owed it, not because they are _entitled_ to it. They get what they want because of _who_ they are, not because of what they _do_." The receptionist described above suffers from a serious case of *entitlement*. Bardwick finds an attitude of entitlement especially prevalent among workers who never reach their full career potential. I find it prevalent among people who have derailed.

A person who has a can-do attitude is not to be confused with a yes-person. Whereas a yes-person acts to please others in an effort to ward off criticism or garner the favor of others, the person with a can-do attitude acts in ways that further the goals of the company or department. He or she knows that adding value is part of his or her job, not adjunct to it. It's easy to see how you can get caught up doing the basic requirements of your job, without realizing that this often is not enough to assure long-term success. People who avoid premature derailment do something more than their jobs. This is what distinguishes them from their colleagues. They are viewed by their management as adding value based on a contribution over and above what may be contained in their job descriptions, and they understand what it truly means to be of service.

To Be of Service

A common complaint heard today is that "so-and-so acted as though he were doing me a favor when all he did was his job." And it isn't an ill-founded complaint. Whether in a restaurant or schoolroom, at the post office, in a department store, or in your own office, you see people performing the job to which they are assigned act as though they were being put out by requests from the very people they are there to serve. This was certainly the case with our receptionist at the beginning of the chapter. We each perform a service that, presumably, is of value to the company or the customer or we wouldn't be paid to do it. Why, then, do so many people resist providing the best service that they possibly can? Perhaps the answer lies, at least partially, in our interpretation of the word *service* and the fact that it is closely aligned with the word *servant*.

Although none of us likes to think of himself or herself as a servant, Robert K. Greenleaf, a former AT&T executive and founder of the Indianapolis-based Center for Applied Ethics, illuminates another way to think about it. Greenleaf's book, *Servant Leadership: A Journey into the Nature of Legitimate Power and Greatness,* significantly changed my view of the role that I play in serving others. His use of the term *leadership* in the title should be looked at broadly in the context of service, as opposed to simply a reference to those in authority. Even with formal leaders in place in organizations, we each play the role of leader from time to time. The example that Greenleaf uses is the character Leo in Hermann Hesse's *Journey to the East.* Leo is the servant, in the traditional sense, to a group of men who are on a mythical journey. He performs menial tasks for them, but he also is an influential spirit within the group. Leo buoys the men through his powerful presence. When he disappears, the men find that they can't continue the journey without him. Greenleaf writes: "to me, this story clearly says that *the great leader is seen as servant first,* and that simple fact is key to his greatness. Leo was actually the leader all of the time, but he was servant first because that was what he was, *deep down inside.*"

Unfortunately, we have come to regard service as something done by anyone in a lesser position than ours. Even in organizations that claim to be nonhierarchical, a pecking order still exists. It begins with the company president and continues down throughout the organization to entry-level positions. The pecking order dictates who you can have lunch with, be social with, and offer assistance to. It is somewhat ridiculous when you think about it because within any organization everyone is there to serve the customer or client. We are all, then, servants in one way or another. Whether or not we have direct contact with customers, our work affects the final outcome. You frequently hear line people describe staff people as "overhead." Staff people (also called "back office" or "corporate") don't directly contribute to developing, producing, or selling a product or service, so they are not thought of as contributing to the bottom line. Staff people, however, provide valuable services to line people—services without which the product or service could not be produced as efficiently or effectively.

This point was beautifully illustrated at yet another leadership program held at the Ritz-Carlton in Pasadena, California. To make the point about the importance of a can-do attitude, I asked if two of the maintenance men responsible for setting up the room would answer some questions about why they provide such high-quality service. Participants asked these men questions to help them better understand the can-do attitude exhibited by all the staff's employees.

Q: *Why do you think you provide service so superior to that of your counterparts at other hotels?*

A: Because we're treated so well. We're trained that we are ladies and gentlemen serving ladies and gentlemen. When we pass another employee in the hall, it's expected that we will treat that person the same as we would an important guest.

Q: *Do you think that how you set up this room has any effect on the profits of the hotel?*

A: Yes. If we put a tablecloth on that is stained, and you lift your glass and find the stain, then you'll look at that all day and remember it when you're deciding whether or not to come back and stay with us.

Q: *How is it that you deliver even the most obscure requests?*

A: We're each given a budget so that if a guest asks for something that we don't have, we can go out and buy it. All we have to do is present the receipt to the boss and we're paid back by the hotel.

Q: *You mean you can just leave the hotel, get in your car, and go down to Office Depot and buy what we need?*

A: Yes. After we tell our supervisor that we're going.

If you examine this notion of serving as Greenleaf does, that "the work exists for the person as much as the person exists for the work—the business then becomes a serving institution—serving those who produce and those who use," then being a servant isn't such a bad thing after all. We each serve others in different, but invaluable, ways. People with a can-do attitude understand that their positions exist to serve the customer as well as their colleagues.

I once walked past the employee lounge in a department store and saw a posted sign that read: "People are not an interruption of our work—they *are* our work." It was a simple sign, but one that I never forgot. It acted as a reminder to employees that their role was to serve others. A can-do attitude is prevalent in those who understand this very basic premise. Can you imagine working in a company where the executives see themselves as servants? Or in a school where the principal sees himself or herself as there to serve the teachers and students? How might it change the environment? Would their constituents think any less of them? On the contrary—it would create an enhanced sense of teamwork and customer-driven behavior.

Here is a list of some of the most common complaints that I hear about the absence of a can-do attitude. You can decide which ones may apply to you.

• **WORKS TO RULE.** Does just enough work to get by—doesn't do anything extra or beyond the scope of his or her job description.

• **NOT A SELF-STARTER.** Does the work to which he or she is specifically assigned, but doesn't seek additional responsibility or see what else needs to be done unless told, and even then requires an inordinate amount of supervision.

- **RESISTANT TO NEW IDEAS.** Prefers doing things in routine ways and is unwilling to consider new methods for improving the quality or quantity of work.
- **NOT A TEAM PLAYER.** Does only his or her own work—doesn't help out others in a pinch.
- **LACKS ENTHUSIASM.** Does the job, but without excitement or energy.
- **UNCOOPERATIVE.** Fails to help implement or may sabotage new ideas that others generate for improving products or services.
- **UNMOTIVATED.** Meets not even the basic job requirements and requires constant prodding or coaxing.
- **BAD ATTITUDE.** This is usually a catchall term for a generally negative, critical, or condescending approach to customer service or team efforts.

If you see yourself in one or more of these terms, then you must seriously consider why this is the case—and do something about it. Let's take a look at why people fail to exhibit a can-do attitude.

Why No-Can-Do?

By now, it should be no surprise to you that I do not believe that people are born with a lack of service orientation. They develop it—and for good reasons. Whether it is developed as a childhood defense mechanism in response to unreasonable demands or as a method for dealing with ineffective leadership, it will quickly derail the best of employees before they realize it. An understanding of why and how it develops can help you to overcome a no-can-do attitude.

1. **POOR MANAGEMENT.** Although managers are often quick to point the finger at employees who lack a can-do attitude, they fail to realize that they themselves may be the cause of it. The most common ways in which managers curb enthusiasm and motivation are to be too controlling or overly critical. If you are a manager, remember to delegate the *project* not the *process*. When managers control how someone does something, they eventually succeed in having everything done their way, but their way may not always be the best way. It only serves to thwart creativity and innovation. Similarly, overly critical managers make staff members afraid to show initiative for fear of being unjustly criticized for their efforts. In either case, employees eventually wait to be told what to do, how to do it, and brace themselves for anticipated disapproval.

2. **POOR JOB MATCH.** Countless people are in jobs for which they are ill suited because they were steered into them by well-meaning parents or teachers, or because they can't see the options available to them. High salaries, family expectations, prestige, and other perks and benefits keep people in jobs they hate going to each day. These reasons become what are known as "golden handcuffs." People dislike the work, but remain tied to it because of social or financial reasons. As a result, they suffer from lackluster performance and low motivation. It is pretty difficult to enthusiastically perform a job you just don't like.

3. **POWERLESS/POWERFUL PARENTING.** Either end of the power spectrum can impede a child from developing a healthy sense of initiative. On the one hand, when parents present themselves as all-powerful, it is tough for the child to think he or she knows the right thing to do; instead, he looks to authority for the answers. The old maxims "father knows best" and "children are to be seen and not heard" summarize what is at the root of these behaviors. Employees who won't make a move without being given permission or direction may have had parents who expected them

to be compliant and submissive. On the other hand, parents who see themselves as lacking control over their own lives often instill the same in their children. Parents who allow themselves to be controlled by the desires of others may unwittingly impart the message to their children that their lot in life is to follow the instructions given to them and not make waves with their own ideas or methods for doing things. As adults, people who had either powerless or powerful parenting may lack the necessary confidence to take the kind of risks required to extend themselves beyond what is asked.

4. **HIGH DETAIL ORIENTATION.** What strategic thinkers call resistance to new ideas may in actuality be a manifestation of high detail orientation. Such people often see only the complexities of an idea and retort with the many reasons why it can't possibly work, instead of seeking solutions to those barriers that are less obvious to the big-picture person. They become overwhelmed by the morass of details required to make a new idea a reality and are unable to break it into smaller, manageable pieces.

5. **MONOPOLY OF PRODUCTS OR SERVICES.** The absence of competition can lead to a "take-it-or-leave-it" mentality. Whether it's the only grocery store in a small town or the only provider of air transportation out of a particular city, a monopoly can serve to diminish the attention paid to and value placed on customer service. People working in a monopolistic organization tend to forget that they are there to serve others and instead take advantage of their position in the market.

6. **DEPRESSION.** The incidence of depression in the U.S. population is far greater than most people realize. Statistics suggest that women have a 20 to 26 percent lifetime risk for depression and men an 8 to 12 percent lifetime risk. Symptoms of depression include, among others, the loss of interest in activities one normally finds enjoyable and feelings of general fatigue or lethargy. Depression is a significant factor that can contribute to one's lack

of enthusiasm or motivation to perform the job in anything more than a perfunctory manner. In order to address the appropriate cause, it is important to understand that the work can contribute to the depression as well as the depression contribute to failure to perform the work.

No matter how difficult it may be for you to do so, exhibiting a positive, upbeat, can-do attitude is yet another factor critical to avoiding premature career derailment. It doesn't mean that you have to do everything that is asked of you, regardless of the reasonableness of the request; it simply means that you take a positive approach to work, serving the customer, and meeting unforeseen challenges. With the exception of an abrasive personality, the absence of a can-do attitude is easier to spot than any of the other derailment factors described heretofore. This is what makes it such a critical ingredient in your repertoire of skills.

Ways to Exhibit a Can-Do Attitude

Certain companies provide outstanding examples of the presence of a can-do attitude. One such company is the Four Seasons hotel chain. A number of years ago, I was caught in a snowstorm in Boston that began on a Friday morning. I was staying at the Four Seasons and was hesitant to check out for fear of not getting another room in the city if the storm persisted. The desk clerk assured me that there would be no problem. Knowing that "no problem" can mean anything from just that to "really big problem," I remained worried and skeptical throughout the day. By four o'clock that afternoon, Logan Airport had been closed, and I trudged through the snow back to the hotel. While I waited in line behind irate would-be guests demanding rooms that just weren't available, I noticed that the same woman who had earlier promised that there would be no problem was still there. I dreaded what I was sure I was about to hear. When my turn came and I stepped up to the desk, she smiled and said, "Welcome back, Dr. Frankel. When I heard the airport was closed I went ahead and checked you in. Here's your key."

I was more than just a little impressed by the woman's service orientation. She delivered exactly what she said she would—and a bit more. She could have made me feel fortunate to even have a room, given the fact that she could have sold it several times over, but she didn't. She made me feel like a welcome guest. In our respective fields, we are all capable of providing this kind of service, but most of us don't, despite the fact that it's what builds successful companies and contributes to successful careers. Instead, we rely on our technical competence and assume that it will get us over the rough spots. Then, we scratch our heads with wonder when we are passed over for promotions or developmental opportunities.

A second example of a can-do attitude is that of a company that redefined service in the retail clothes marketing arena: Nordstrom. Despite the fact that the company is a high-end concern, it flourished financially even in down markets in no small part because of the customer service attitude exhibited by its sales associates. When you shop at Nordstrom, you are usually met by friendly, knowledgeable, and helpful staff. Without being particularly pushy or aggressive, they make certain that you find what you are looking for. Long before Nordstrom's competitors were doing it, the company had a full return policy—no questions asked, your money was refunded. Countless times I've heard people say that even though Nordstrom costs a bit more they continue shopping there because of the service they receive. I wonder how many people can say that *their* customers exhibit the same loyalty for the products or services they offer.

Then there are the companies that, rightly or wrongly, are notorious for the absence of a service mentality. The only way that they stay in business is by offering a specialized product or service.

The U.S. Postal Service is a case in point. With over a half-million employees nationwide, the Postal Service is the largest employer in the country and, until recently, offered products and services that no one else did. Giving credit where credit is due, postal employees perform the herculean task of moving massive amounts of mail around the country, in a timely fashion, at a reasonable cost, and with a very low percentage of letters or packages becoming lost. Now that they are given the choice, however, consumers have flocked to alternative sources for express mail service—despite the fact that the Postal Service offers the same service and at a more reasonable price. Why? In part because of the attitudes of some postal employees.

The topic of discussion at a recent neighborhood party was just this problem. There are four post offices within a three-mile radius of our neighborhood. As it turned out, most of us said that when we had the time, we went to the one farthest away because it had the friendliest staff. At the same time, everyone could name the surliest people at the other locations. The Postal Service provides an outstanding example of how poor management and, in many cases, a poor job match combine to create a no-can-do attitude that is noticeable to all who frequent an establishment. In this case, the fact that no one else manufactures or sells postage stamps or delivers routine letters surely affects customer service. Now, if a group of neighbors spend time talking about something as mundane as where they buy their stamps, what might they be saying about the product or service offered by *your* company based on *your* attitude?

There are seven specific things that you can do to assure that you are perceived as someone with a can-do attitude. I preface them by saying that logic and common sense must prevail when responding to any request. There are people who constantly demand unreasonable things of you, and to always have a can-do attitude with these people may be unrealistic or even inappropriate. The customer is *not* always right. You are not expected to be a doormat. On the other hand, you should consider the effect your attitude has on customers, clients, and colleagues and how you can be a better ambassador for the product or services that you provide.

QUESTION/REQUEST	NO-CAN-DO RESPONSE	CAN-DO RESPONSE
Do you think that you'll be able to meet the client's deadline?	I'm not sure. There are an awful lot of obstacles that make it look unlikely.	I have a few concerns, but nothing that can't be overcome if we put our heads together.
Can I exchange this pair of pants for a sweater?	There are no returns or exchanges on sale items.	It is not within the scope of my authority to approve the request, but let me see if I can find someone who can.
Because Todd is on vacation I'd like you to prepare the monthly status report for the president.	Well . . . I've never done it before. I'm not sure I know how.	Sure. I've never done it before but I'm sure I can figure it out. If I have any questions I'll ask.
Would you take a look at these recommendations for changes to our product delivery system and give me your input?	I don't know what's wrong with our old system. Besides, it will take at least six months to get it up and running and we've got a new product line coming out around the same time.	I'd be happy to. If we're going to make any changes, this is a good time, since it will take six months to get it up and running and we've got a new product line coming out just after that.

QUESTION/REQUEST	NO-CAN-DO RESPONSE	CAN-DO RESPONSE
Would you mind processing this expense report for me today because I'm leaving town again tomorrow?	We only process expense reports on Fridays. You'll have to wait until you get back to get your money. Besides, this isn't filled in correctly. You'll have to go back and change it.	We normally process those checks on Fridays, but I don't think that there will be a problem making an exception for you. I did notice that it's missing some necessary information. Why don't I show you what's needed.
We need someone to train the new person on Windows. Would you mind doing it?	I'm not a trainer, you know. I'll need an outline of the goals and objectives before I start and someone else to relieve me of my duties for the six hours that it's going to take.	I've never trained anyone on it before, but I'm willing to give it a try if she'll be patient with me.
I've never used your services before. I was wondering whether you could help me to understand what's available?	What is it that you need to know?	I'd be happy to. Which services in particular were you interested in, or would you like me to go over all of them?
I need some information for tomorrow's presentation by 4:00 P.M. today.	You've got to be kidding. Why is everything around here an emergency?	I don't think I'll be of much help because I'm already on a high-priority project. Let's find another way to get it done on time.

1. **DEVELOP SELF-CONFIDENCE.** Each of the following suggestions is predicated on the presence of a healthy degree of self-confidence. A can-do attitude stems from a belief in yourself and your abilities. It isn't a false sense of confidence, but rather one that comes from the knowledge that even when you're unsure of yourself, you know from past successes and accomplishments that you can do this too—and if you can't, you will find someone who can help. By exhibiting self-confidence, we often find that we can do more than we originally thought or learn something that will be useful in the future. In essence, we stretch ourselves to the limits of our abilities.

It appears to me that men tend to have more of an edge than women when it comes to exhibiting self-confidence in new or challenging situations. For example, when a job or assignment comes open for which a woman has no direct experience, she will often decline it, or fail to apply for it, because she thinks she can't do it. In the same situation, men tend to jump in wholeheartedly with the confidence that they'll figure it out as they go along.

Regardless of their sex, people who approach assignments and challenges with confidence instill in others a sense of confidence in them. They are perceived as performers who can handle any task, creatively solve problems, and add value to a department or company.

2. **CREATE WIN-WIN SITUATIONS.** Success in creating win-win situations has a lot to do with managing the impressions that others have of you. You want to convey the message that you are ready, willing, and able to help—even when on the inside you're not sure how you're going to do it. When it's clear that you can't do something that you've been asked to do, you turn it into a win-win by helping to find an alternative solution. Consider how changing one's response in each of the situations given in the chart could make a significant difference in the perception of a can-do versus a no-can-do attitude.

3. **DELIVER WHAT YOU PROMISE—AND MORE.** It never ceases to amaze me how many people fail to deliver what they say they will. Although there are myriad reasons why people don't come through with what they've promised, not many of them are good ones. You may know people who have a can-do attitude but who don't produce what they've committed to. The natural corollary to meeting or beating deadlines is assuring that you don't promise *more than* you can deliver. Building contractors are notorious for having a can-do attitude, then not delivering. No matter how specifically you explain your requirements and closely supervise them, it seems that they finish the job late and over budget. They either underestimate the time required or the complexity of the task, and then they wind up falling short on delivering what they promise. Once this happens, their credibility is seriously damaged. As a result, you see contractors going out of business at a fairly high rate.

Going the extra mile to meet, or even beat, a deadline pays huge dividends in the long run. If it means that you have to work late, come in early, or skip lunch, then so be it. This is not to say that you should miss some important event such as your child's recital, your spouse's birthday, or a parent's anniversary in order to deliver what you promise. Rather, you must anticipate these events vis-à-vis your commitments and make certain that they are *all* met. It means that you must *realistically* plan your work and work your plan.

A common complaint heard from managers is that employees seem to lack the commitment to get the job done within predetermined deadlines. One client called bemoaning the fact that one of her best staff members comes in late and takes extended lunch hours, despite the fact that a particular project is already past due and her client is awaiting the results. Regardless of the employee's technical competence, his failure to deliver on his promises is derailing him more than he realizes. The person with a can-do attitude does whatever it takes to get the job done on time and under budget.

Delivering more than you promise serves to add chips to your account. For example, if you say you'll prepare an outline for an upcoming project, why not include more specifics than typically required, such as costs, a detailed methodology, and ways to overcome anticipated obstacles. If you are known as someone who does not only what you promise but more, then those occasional times when something prevents you from meeting an obligation are overlooked or tolerated (the key word being *occasional*). You have built credibility that fares well for you in the long term.

4. **ANTICIPATE REQUIREMENTS.** It is often difficult for people who are detail oriented to foresee ancillary requirements or peripheral issues that will affect the completion of a project. They may be great at checking things off their written or mental lists, but if it's not on the list it doesn't get done. It is a bit like the situation mentioned in the previous chapter in which someone is instructed to cancel plane reservations but neglects to cancel related hotel and car arrangements. The person with a can-do attitude goes above and beyond what is specifically requested by considering all related factors and responding to them in advance.

I once appeared for an all-day training session in a client's office to find the office manager stewing over the fact that the person responsible for scheduling the training room had neglected to order the food for the meeting. When I asked whether she had specifically told the person that she wanted food ordered, she said, "I shouldn't have to. Every time we have an all-day meeting we have food. She should have known to do it." Although it could be argued that the manager shouldn't expect the person to read her mind, her expectation that this staff member will anticipate her needs, especially in light of the fact that a certain protocol is typically followed, isn't unreasonable.

Unfortunately, the old adage "If I knew better, I'd do better" holds true here. If someone isn't particularly good at anticipating requirements, it makes it difficult for him or her to do it. Many of the coaching hints suggested under Reason #6 for developing a better sense of the bigger picture hold true here. In particular, before beginning or completing a project or response to a request, take the time to think about it in its entirety. If you're not sure of what may be required in addition to the obvious, ask questions—particularly of people who are better than you at seeing the big picture.

5. **OFFER HELP FREELY—DON'T WAIT TO BE ASKED.** Failure to offer to help does not always stem from a withholding or stingy personality, although it certainly can. People who are reticent to offer help often are afraid to be intrusive or overstep their boundaries. It reminds me of the person who watches as someone struggles to get through a door with an armload of packages, whereas someone else hurries to help open the door. It goes back to the need for a generosity of spirit.

A can-do attitude doesn't only mean that you can do your own job, it means that you have the best interest of the organization in mind and work to achieve its goals as well as yours. You may have worked with people who leave the office when their work is completed, even when they see others in their group or department working late to meet a deadline. It may not occur to them to offer help, or they may think that it isn't their job. Keep in mind that the job is to best serve the customer. This means that your work isn't limited by your specific job description.

6. **ALWAYS OFFER A SOLUTION, OR REQUEST ASSISTANCE IN FINDING A SOLUTION, TO IDENTIFIED PROBLEMS.** Managers frequently express frustration with people whom they perceive as malcontents or troublemakers. They describe such people as those who complain about their workload, coworkers, or the injustice of a system that overworks and underpays, but who make no effort to do anything about it. Their whining and complaints bring down the morale of the entire office or department.

People with a can-do attitude, on the other hand, assume responsibility for making things better by pairing any complaint that they may have with suggested solutions or requests for assistance with finding a solution. They don't complain for the sake of complaining, but rather openly discuss problems with the parties concerned in an effort to make things better. If they can't find a solution to the problem themselves, they ask for help in finding one. They know that if things are going to get better, it will be because of their willingness to meet problems head-on.

This guideline is particularly pertinent for team building. People will grumble to one another in small groups about problems in the department, but seldom do they see improving the situation as their responsibility. Once it is made a norm for everyone on the team to assume responsibility, rather than only the manager or team leader, then entire departments move forward with a surge of new ideas and solutions to old problems. It won't work, however, if the team leader fails to empower team members and still expects them to resolve team problems. Success, in this regard, is contingent on the collective wisdom and energy that spring from groups of people who work collaboratively toward a common goal.

7. **DO WHAT YOU LOVE—NOT ONLY WHAT YOU'RE GOOD AT.** Doing what you love can contribute not only to the ability to think more broadly, but also to a can-do attitude. When you do what you love, you quite naturally want to be of service and share your enthusiasm with others. There's no problem that becomes insurmountable when you approach your work with passion.

If you're lucky, what you love and what you're good at are one and the same, but this is not always true. I know a surgeon who is brilliant in his field. He has a full practice and is trusted by his patients and admired by his colleagues for his skill. He once confided in me that he hates his work and, unfortunately, this is reflected in his attitude toward his patients. It is not uncommon to hear them complain about his curtness and dour attitude. Given a choice, many patients say that they would prefer another physician. He's a good example of someone who avoids derailment primarily because his skill is so specialized that he has no local competition.

A man with whom I used to work left the company at about the same time that I did to start his own business. Nearly two years after we were each on our own, we were talking about how quickly the days and weeks fly by now that we're doing what we love. His comment "My worst day on my own is better than my best day working for someone else" frequently resonates in my mind because it's true. Whether you work for someone else or for yourself, you know when you're doing what you love because the challenges are easier to meet and the positive attitude with which you approach your work is obvious to all those with whom you interact.

Some readers may now be thinking, "Doing what you love is easier said than done." From the surgeon who stays in practice for the money to the engineer who needs the health insurance that the job provides to his family, people become stuck in careers for which they no longer have enthusiasm. Social, family, and financial pressures keep people in unsatisfying jobs long after they have stopped enjoying their work and being productive. Feeling stuck contributes to lackluster performance and can also be one cause of depression and physical ailments. The belief that you have no options and are instead constricted by considerations outside of your control is frequently a factor in depression.

You may never have thought of yourself as depressed, but think about these questions:

- Have you given up after-work activities in which you were once interested because you lack energy to engage in them?
- Do you find yourself coming alive on Friday afternoon and becoming more morose on Sunday afternoon with the thought of the next day being a workday?

- Do you pace yourself, in terms of expenditure of energy, so that you can get through the week?
- Do you find yourself frequently daydreaming at work or unable to concentrate on the task at hand?
- Are vacations the highlight of your life?
- Do you catch colds easily and find yourself complaining about a host of aches and pains (either real or imagined)?
- Do you exceed your allowable sick days at work?
- Do you use alcohol or other substances to camouflage your feelings about work?

If you answer yes to any of these questions, it may be that you are in the wrong job and that your situation is making you more depressed than you realize. It is important that you objectively assess your situation and determine ways in which you can balance your obligations with a fulfilling career or outside interests. Talk to friends and family members about your dreams and aspirations and ask for their input. Speak with a career counselor. Interview other people who have successfully moved from an unrewarding job to one they now love. Once you do, you may find that you're not as stuck as you thought you were and that you have more support than you thought for making a career move.

About a year ago, a man named Brett asked me to coach him. At our first meeting, he described what seemed to be a wonderful job that he had as the chief financial officer at a midsize company. He reported that there were no problems with his supervisor that he couldn't handle, and announced that his pay and benefits exceeded his expectations. What then, I asked, could I possibly do for him? As it turned out, Brett was bored with his job and didn't feel that he was using the skills he valued most—working with his hands in the building trades. After exploring possible opportunities within his company, it quickly became clear that there were no jobs inside the company that would be any more appealing to him than the one he had. When it appeared that he would have to begin a job search outside the company, he said that this wasn't possible. His wife was in a low-paying job, and he bore the burden of supporting the family, his in-laws, and two residences. Brett felt like he was stuck.

Our work together focused on getting Brett to talk to his wife about his dreams, to a financial planner about how much the family *needed* to live on, as opposed to what they were living on, and to begin investigating the possibilities in the field where he would be most happy. He wasn't expected to make any moves right away, just plant seeds that might grow to fruition over time. It turned out that his wife was incredibly supportive—more so than he had anticipated. The financial planner gave him good ideas for how he could save money and areas in the country where he might be able to live more economically than where he currently resided. As a result of his legwork, Brett came up with a two-year plan for leaving the company and moving toward a career that would be more rewarding for him and enable him to spend more time with his family. He has another year to go before he actually leaves, but the past months have been a breeze for him at work because he knows he has a plan in place that will soon free him from the golden handcuffs.

The preceding example is intended to illustrate that you may not be as constricted as you think. Existential philosophers say that two of our greatest burdens in life are freedom and responsibility. Even in the most dire circumstances, we have the freedom to choose how we will handle the situation—and the responsibility to deal consciously with that choice. Staying in a job that you no longer like or that positively depresses you is a choice. Before you settle for that choice be certain that you have explored creative alternatives for living your life differently. Not only is your well-being at stake, but the well-being of your family as well.

The importance of having a can-do attitude should by now be abundantly clear. People with a can-do attitude attract similar people and positive experiences. The world works in synchronicity with the person who has a positive, upbeat attitude. Managers report that when interviewing job candidates, a can-do attitude is often weighed more heavily than technical competence. They know that they can teach the basics of a job to someone, but they can't teach someone to have a positive attitude.

Ways to Develop a Can-Do Attitude

1. Always deliver *more* than you promise.
2. Never miss a deadline—and when possible to do so without sacrificing quality, beat it.
3. Replace initial skepticism with creative problem solving.
4. Always accompany a complaint with a proposed solution or a request for assistance with finding a solution.
5. Leave your bad moods outside the office.
6. Actively search for ways to better serve the customer or client.
7. Regardless of your job title, view yourself as both a servant and as a leader.
8. Make certain that you're doing work that you love—even if it means carving a niche within the scope of less enjoyable work.
9. Volunteer for unusual or nonroutine assignments.

10. Use free time to develop systems that add value to the customer or company.

11. When appropriate—lighten up. Smile. Make it fun for others to work with you.

12. Seek help for depression.

13. Return all phone calls, regardless of whom they are from, in a timely manner.

14. Respond to requests with a time frame for completion—don't leave people guessing about what you're going to do and when you plan to do it.

15. Help others overcome their barriers to success.

16. Realistically assess what you can or can't do and don't promise more than you can deliver.

17. Turn lose-lose situations into win-win ones by looking for opportunities to negotiate.

18. Make saying that something can't be done the exception rather than the rule.

19. Carefully listen to the needs of your customers and make certain that what you deliver matches what they need.

20. Go the extra mile by broadly defining your responsibilities rather than performing within the bounds of a narrow job description.

21. If you can't figure out how something can be done, get someone who can to help you.

22. When your work is done, and sometimes even when it isn't, offer to help others with theirs.

23. Use positive self-talk to tape over messages that diminish your self-confidence.

24. Learn as much as you can about how your work contributes to your company's bottom-line profits or services.

Working in Isolation

NETWORK FOR SUCCESS

The training manager at a large firm requested that a networking program be developed as an in-house course. The manager thought that it was important for employees to understand the significance of networking for on-the-job success and how to network more effectively. After the program was advertised in the firm's internal newsletter, only eight people signed up to take it—all women. Despite the small class size, it was decided that the two-day program would proceed as planned. At the end of the first day, the women commented on how helpful the information was and that they were learning a lot about the subject. The women were asked their opinions as to why, if the information was so beneficial, more people didn't sign up for the program. One woman said that she tried to talk a male coworker into taking the class with her, but that he laughed and said, "Networking? That's just a bunch of women standing around in high heels sipping white wine."

The impression that networking is only for women or members of a specific group, or that it is in some way manipulative, ignores what men have always practiced. Long before it was called networking, men gathered together to exchange war stories and undoubtedly other information pertinent to how to succeed in business by really trying. That was referred to as *the old boys' club*. Vestiges of the old boys' club remain in some cities where private facilities still exist that enable male executives to assemble for meals, meetings, or a drink after work. The men who belong to these facilities are, in effect, networking.

With the proliferation of information technology, and the increasingly popular movement toward team-based efforts, individuals are no longer expected to perform their job responsibilities in isolation. The Internet is testimony to this fact. Whereas in the past people worked independently on projects and were by and large rewarded for their individual contributions, today's worker is expected to function interdependently with a large base of information accessible through his or her relationships with others. Harvard professor John Kotter has conducted extensive research into the factors that contribute to success as a general manager. One of his findings, that a strong network is an essential ingredient of managerial effectiveness, holds true not only for managers, but for people at *all* levels in an organization. Kotter describes a network as *the sum total of the people, both inside and outside your organization, on whom you depend to get your job done.* As was already emphasized under Reason #1, building relationships is critical to creating an effective network. The people who prematurely derail are often the same ones who fail to understand, build, and nurture their professional networks.

Assess your networking acumen with the following checklist.

_____ I belong to professional groups related to my field and am actively involved in them.

_____ I can specifically name the people in my network.

_____ I know what I have to offer others in my network.

_____ I don't view networking as a waste of time, but rather
as an invaluable tool for assuring ongoing success.

_____ I spend some portion of each week engaged in at least
one networking activity.

_____ I freely share expertise, information, or another
commodity with those in my network.

_____ I feel comfortable calling on others in my network
and asking for help when I need it.

_____ I can honestly say that my work is made easier
because of my network relationships.

_____ I have network relationships at all levels of my
organization as well as outside of it.

_____ At times, I use informal gatherings as an opportunity
to network.

_____ I'm known as someone who helps others to "connect"
professionally.

From Organization Charts to Networks

In the old scheme of things, we used to refer to organization charts
to determine where we fell in the pecking order. Hierarchical by
design, they typically looked something like the chart presented
on page 216. Organizational charts provided order to the workforce but did so in a manner that preserved the ranking system,
created vertical fiefdoms, and discouraged interdepartmental de-
pendencies.

Today it is more helpful, and appropriate, to think of yourself
at the center of a complex web of people, both inside and outside
of your organization, with whom you interact in an effort to get
the job done effectively. Although some facets of the hierarchy remain, the boundaries between organizational levels have become
less clear and crossing them (intentionally and otherwise) is more
acceptable while trying to accomplish interrelated tasks. The dia-

gram on page 217 exemplifies how you might now look at your network. It takes Kotter's concept of the manager's network, described in his work *The General Managers* (The Free Press, 1982), and expands it to include any position within an organization. As you can see, in this new configuration, you are central to the interconnecting web of relationships required to successfully meet the organization's goals. With so many relationships to manage, you can also see why building and maintaining relationships is a factor critical to avoiding career derailment.

Networking is nothing more than simple cognizance of the fact that every person with whom you come into contact is potentially helpful, or harmful, to your success. The moment you enter into a discussion with a colleague about a mutual project, you are networking. When you meet someone at a party whose company uses the same products or services that your company provides, you are networking. The caveat is, you can't build a network for only selfish purposes. People will see through it if you do. You must approach your network relationships in the same manner as you do other relationships—with a generosity of spirit and genuine desire to help, and be helped by, others. At the moment you build a relationship, you are never certain whether you will help it or be helped by it. Remember, *when you need a relationship, it is too late to build it.*

Who Needs to Network?

Even people who are willing to change their behaviors in significant ways in order to avoid career derailment seem to resist networking and come up with a plethora of excuses for avoiding it. These concerns are addressed below.

Excuse #1: *I'm not a good networker.*
Response: Not one of us emerged from the womb a good networker. Although some people are better at it than others,

most of us have to make a concerted effort to build relationships. As with other relationships, networking requires certain social skills and comfort with being with others. One tactic that makes networking easier is to use the active listening techniques described under Reason #1. Most people love it when others ask them questions and really listen to their responses. If necessary, take the Dale Carnegie course in how to make friends and influence people. The fact of the matter is, the more you network the easier it becomes.

Excuse #2: *It's a waste of my company's time and money.*

Response: Not true. The knowledge, goodwill, or potential business that you gain from networking is highly beneficial to your company. Through networking relationships you increase the pool of resources you may need in the future. Similarly, by acting as a resource for others outside your firm, you

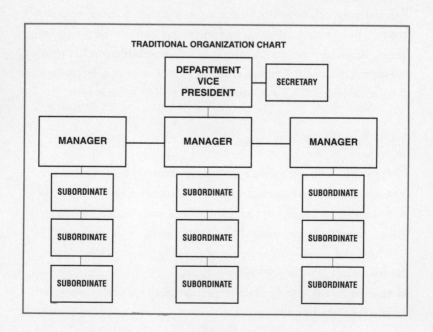

TRADITIONAL ORGANIZATION CHART

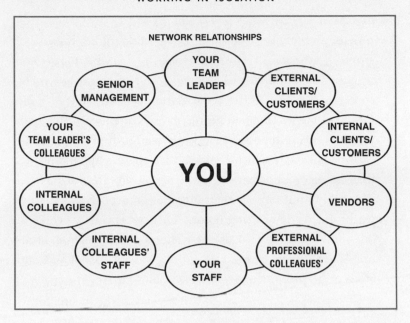

indirectly call attention to your company's products or service. Even internal networking pays dividends in terms of the productivity, brainstorming, and cost savings that result from increased cooperation between teams and individuals over time.

Excuse #3: *My workload doesn't permit it.*

Response: Your workload may not permit it because you *don't* network. If your schedule is so heavy that you don't have time to network, it may just be that you aren't effectively pooling resources and building bridges of collaboration with internal and external colleagues. Instead, you wind up reinventing the wheel. You must view networking not as an option, but as a *responsibility.* It is your responsibility to have in place any relationships that can further the attainment of your company's, and your own, goals.

Excuse #4: *I already have plenty of contacts.*

Response: Except in cases where one's work suffers because of spending too much time networking, in which case you wouldn't be using this excuse, you can never have too many contacts. Go back to the networking chart on page 217 and fill in the names of actual people in each category with whom you actively build positive working relationships. If any of the categories have few or no names, then these may be the areas that require your attention. Some people are great at internal networking but neglect their outside contacts. This situation works until a downsizing occurs. Others, especially people in sales and marketing, focus their efforts on external networking. The numbers look great, but often at the cost of a painful effort at getting the internal work achieved.

Excuse #5: *Networking is manipulative.*

Response: It is only as manipulative as you make it. If you network only for what you can get out of it personally, then it probably is manipulative. On the other hand, if you remember the quid pro quo of relationships—something in exchange for something else—then you are more likely to see and acknowledge opportunities for helping others when they arise. Whether you care to admit it, you are networking every time you meet someone. I'm only putting a name to what happens when people enter into mutually beneficial or rewarding relationships. There is no doubt that you gain personally and professionally from networking. It typically isn't an act of altruism, but it also isn't such a bad thing. Everyone walks away a winner when networking is done properly.

How Networking Works

Every interaction is a networking opportunity. The benefit or quid pro quo may not at first be clear, and it may *never* materialize; nevertheless, networking is important in building positive workplace relationships. Networking can be the difference between making and losing a career. A case in point is the brouhaha caused early in Clinton's presidency by naming his wife, Hillary, as chair of the White House task force on health care issues. The commotion can, at least in part, be ascribed to the fact that prior to the appointment Hillary had few allies in Washington. The Clintons were relative outsiders. There is no doubt that the First Lady could capably handle the assignment, but she had no network in place to support the unprecedented decision.

What do you think would have happened if Bob Dole, as president, had given the same assignment to his wife, Elizabeth? I believe that the outcome would have been quite different. Mrs. Dole is a well-connected, well-respected Washington insider, known for, among other things, her work as president of the Red Cross and secretary of labor during the Bush administration. In contrast to Hillary Clinton, Elizabeth Dole has developed and maintained a role appropriate network.

On the other hand, Lee Iacocca's success at turning around Chrysler was due, in part, to two key factors: bringing in a new management team and securing government funds to bail out the carmaker. Iacocca was able to do both not only because of his track record at Ford, but also because of the relationships that he already had in place when he arrived at Chrysler. He once said that building relationships did not come naturally to him early in his career. It initially made him feel uncomfortable and awkward, but he knew it was important and persevered at it in the same way he did each of his other goals.

People who fail to network, or see it as superfluous to their primary tasks, miss out on untold opportunities. Networking provides you access to inside information about upcoming trends in your business, client leads, information essential to accomplishing your work, assistance with special projects, and myriad other benefits. Often, the networking process isn't obvious and the benefits may not be realized until long after a relationship is established.

Here is an example. A woman I will call Rachael worked with me in the same corporation for a number of years. When I left the company to start my own business, she remained. Although we initially had intermittent contact, communication dwindled until there was no contact. After several years with no contact, Rachael called me. It turned out that she had decided to leave the company to start her own consulting business and she wanted to meet with me to discuss the ups and downs of entrepreneurship. We did meet on several occasions and spoke on the phone as Rachael got her business started.

After approximately one year in business for herself, Rachael decided she wasn't cut out for it. She missed the collegiality of working in a large firm as well as the steady income and benefits afforded by it. She took a job with a growing company. As the company grew, opportunities for a consultant with my skills began to emerge. Although she couldn't promise anything, Rachael arranged for me to meet with the people requiring services such as mine. Based on her recommendation, the company began to use my company for certain programs and services. I now have a wonderful relationship with not only Rachael but many of her colleagues as well, and I feel fortunate, professionally and personally, to call this company a client.

When I initially met with Rachael to assist her with information about starting a business, I had absolutely no idea that it would turn out the way that it did. I didn't consciously say to myself, *You never know how Rachael will be able to help you in the future so you'd better find the time to meet with her.* I only knew that she was a colleague who was asking for help and that I wanted to offer whatever assistance I could. Getting something in return was an unanticipated and pleasant surprise.

Even if you never plan on having your own business, you never know when you might be in the position of looking for a better job, trying to gain access to difficult-to-find information, or requiring assistance with a project. In the end, it always pays to offer help when needed and to build positive professional relationships.

Here are a few other networking success stories.

• Larry decided to take a voluntary separation package from his company. He knew that with the money he received he would have six months to find other, more satisfying work. Within six weeks colleagues from professional associations he belonged to called to let him know about opportunities in their respective companies. He is now considering several offers—all of which came through Larry's network contacts.

• Armando was working on a salary study for his department that entailed getting information from competitors about their salary structures. The project was made easier because of his membership in a professional organization of compensation specialists. In exchange for the information others provided, Armando offered to share his findings and final report with his network colleagues.

• Melissa works for a large corporation and was unhappy in her job but didn't want to leave the company entirely. She spoke with several people with whom she had kept in contact from other divisions and asked them to let her know whether any jobs became available that might provide new challenges for her. She was contacted by the vice president of one division and asked to apply for a job for which he thought she was qualified. Her network relationships enabled her to move into an assignment that is more rewarding—both financially and personally.

• Jacob had an idea that could substantially benefit his manufacturing firm. He explained his idea to his boss, but the boss didn't seem interested. He casually mentioned the idea to one of the company president's direct reports while they were flying home from an out-of-town conference. She thought it warranted attention and arranged for him to make a presentation to her boss. Jacob received a bonus, and public recognition, for his contribution to the company—a contribution made possible through a network relationship.

• Shirley was the administrator for a large commercial property management firm. As such, she had significant contact with building contractors, plumbers, electricians, and so forth and always took care to treat these people with the respect they deserved—something that many of her colleagues neglected. When she left the company to start her own property management firm, her clients were impressed with her ability to get vendors to respond to her requests promptly. Although Shirley's own company is nowhere near the size of her former employer, she is given the same service afforded a large company. She is successful where many of her competitors fail because of the network she built during her career.

Clearly, these and other similar experiences validate the importance and benefit of networking. You don't build network relationships with the intention of benefiting from them, but networking clearly pays dividends.

Characteristics of Effective Networkers

Certain characteristics form the basis for effective networking. People who network well typically possess a combination of the following:

1. **GENUINE INTEREST IN OTHERS.** Having a genuine interest in others is at the core of every good relationship—networking or otherwise. A genuine interest in others is manifested by asking

people about themselves (and listening to the response), exhibiting a desire to be of help to them, seeing what they need without them necessarily telling you, and the willingness to go out of your way to help meet those needs. You can't fake genuine interest in others. If you try to fake it, others will perceive you as manipulative or exploitative.

2. **ABILITY TO PUT OTHERS AT EASE.** If you are uncomfortable in networking situations you can overcome your discomfort by focusing attention on making others comfortable. It gives you a role to play that provides something valuable while assuaging your own anxiety in new or unfamiliar situations. One way you can put others at ease is to show genuine interest in them. Another is to introduce them to others whom you may know in the group. When you are the one who is new to a group, you might consider finding someone who may be sitting or standing alone and beginning a conversation with him or her.

3. **COMMITMENT TO A CAUSE GREATER THAN THEM-SELVES.** Kiwanis and Lions Clubs and chambers of commerce are good examples of groups committed to causes greater than simply promoting the well-being of the members. The boards of directors and operating committees of nonprofit organizations are often committed to the cause to which they volunteer their time. Networking through volunteer activities is a wonderful way to meet new people and contribute something to your community at the same time. Such causes bring people together in a positive and meaningful way without focusing exclusively on the benefits of membership.

4. **WILLINGNESS TO GIVE MORE THAN THEY ANTICIPATE RECEIVING IN RETURN.** You don't network because of what you expect to get from it. You network because you believe in the need to work collaboratively and cooperatively with others. This often means that you find yourself giving more to others in your network than you yourself may be receiving at any given time. As de-

scribed under Reason #1, you want to have an inexhaustible supply of chips in your account, earned by extending yourself to others without concern for what you might get in return. One of the best networkers I know is a Cleveland woman who is well respected in the community for her commitment to various charitable causes. Despite her busy schedule, she spends considerable time sharing her resources with others who ask for advice and information. She gives generously of her time and freely shares with others the knowledge gained through her networking activities.

5. **ABILITY TO ASK FOR WHAT THEY NEED.** I've coached people who generously help others but who never ask for anything in return—even when they need it. This ultimately establishes a scenario where others feel uncomfortable because they view themselves as indebted to the person. Eventually, the relationship suffers because of its lopsided nature. Obviously, you are not going to ask for help when you don't need it, but you have to be willing to let others assist you when it is required. *You* not only gain from their efforts, but you allow *them* to feel good about being able to reciprocate.

6. **ABILITY TO ACT AS A CONDUIT BETWEEN OTHERS.** Good networkers help others connect with the resources that they require. They don't simply build relationships for their own personal use; they also help others to succeed by acting as a referral source. For example, when you run into the woman from Cleveland mentioned earlier, she never fails to introduce you to the many people she knows. When she introduces you, she comments on something flattering about you both; for example, "Lynn Smith, let me introduce you to Steve Wilson. Steve single-handedly prevented my computer system from crashing last April right at tax time. Steve, Lynn knows more about investment strategies than anyone I know." This kind of generosity of spirit displays not only the ability to connect people, but the desire to showcase their talents at the same time.

7. **ABILITY TO REMEMBER PEOPLE, INFORMATION, AND EVENTS.** It does no good to network unless you remember the people that you meet and their unique circumstances or story. It is one thing to listen to someone as he or she tells you that it had been a particularly difficult year because his or her child was diagnosed with cancer. It requires something entirely different to remember this piece of information and ask how the person and the child are doing the next time you meet (or call that person). Remembering what people tell you is the sign of a good listener and of someone who networks not only for personal gain but because of a genuine interest in people as well.

Networking Opportunities

Even though nearly every interaction is a networking opportunity, it is also important to seek experiences that promote networking. Finding organizations or opportunities that blend with your own particular interests makes networking more natural and less burdensome. Ideally, you want to be able to spend time with people you enjoy and engage in activities that are of value to you—not only with people or causes who need you (or vice versa). Once you give it some thought, you will be able to come up with your own outlets for networking, but for now here are some ideas that may be of help.

• *Professional associations.* Nearly every profession has an association of members devoted to furthering knowledge in the field, developing expertise in its membership, and providing a forum for members to exchange ideas and information. Typically, if the association is large enough, it has local chapters in addition to a national body and provides members with benefits such as newsletters, magazines, and bulletin boards.

Everyone should belong to at least one professional association and actively participate in its events by attending meetings, volunteering for committees, and taking part in its conferences and special events. The *Encyclopedia of Associations* (see Resources) contains listings for thousands of organizations, briefly describing each organization, why it was founded, the size of its membership, and its publications. It is well worth a trip to the library to take a look at it. Here are just a few of the associations (some of them obscure) included in it:

> AMERICAN ASSOCIATION OF HANDWRITING ANALYSTS
> SOCIETY FOR COMMERCIAL ARCHEOLOGY
> SOCIETY OF WOOD SCIENCE AND TECHNOLOGY
> NATIONAL ASSOCIATION OF WOMEN IN CONSTRUCTION
> INSTITUTE OF FOOD TECHNOLOGISTS
> INDEPENDENT BANKERS ASSOCIATION OF AMERICA
> AUTOMOTIVE SERVICE INDUSTRY ASSOCIATION
> BLACK DATA PROCESSING ASSOCIATES
> NATIONAL COSMETOLOGY ASSOCIATION
> AMERICAN ELECTRONICS ASSOCIATION

If you're the kind of person who would have a hard time joining a professional association alone, do one of two things. First, check around your office to find out if anyone else belongs to the kind of organization you are seeking to join. If not, ask whether anyone else is interested in joining you in attending an association meeting. This may provide you and your colleagues with the opportunity for catching up outside the office while engaging in a mutual interest.

• *Nonprofit organization boards or committees.* Nonprofit organizations are frequently in search of committed people to join their boards of directors or to serve as members of functional committees. They typically look for businesspeople who have skill in one or more specific areas such as fund-raising, finance, human resources, or a related technical field. By becoming involved with a nonprofit organization, you can make a valuable contribution to your community while gaining access to influential people in the community, learning more about the community itself, and developing skills in networking.

There are a number of ways to find out where opportunities for nonprofit involvement lie. Depending on your interests, try making these contacts for starters:

- your company's foundation or human resources department
- the YWCA or YMCA
- your church's pastor or synagogue's rabbi
- the Red Cross
- the board of education or schools in your community
- friends who are involved with nonprofit organizations
- political campaign offices
- the police department
- the chamber of commerce
- hospices
- the Heart Association
- the human interest section of the newspaper
- Big Brothers or Big Sisters of America

- *Special interest clubs.* Networking doesn't have to be all work and no play. There are numerous clubs that cater to nearly every interest imaginable. Whether you like computers, chess, ballroom dancing, hiking, tennis, stamp collecting, or antique cars—there's a club out there waiting for you to join. Choose one that relates to something in which you have an avid interest, and network for fun.

- *Discussion groups.* Many cities have informal groups that gather to discuss recent books, movies, or topics of community interest. They provide a unique opportunity to network while discussing a subject of interest to you. If you can't find one in your town, why not consider starting one? This allows you to play a role instead of just mingling, and is especially helpful for those who are uncomfortable meeting strangers.

• *Informal gatherings.* Have you gotten into a rut where you only go to work and come home, rarely socializing anymore with friends? Why not invite a group of people with whom you share similar interests to join you for a Sunday brunch or dinner? Or, organize a trip to a local museum. Networking can be casual and informal as well as professional and organized. The group may decide to have regular monthly events (hopefully not always at your house) or other weekend activities.

• *Doorway conversations.* Don't forget something as simple and obvious as making a point of dropping by people's offices for a few minutes of casual conversation. If you're uncomfortable with not having a specific purpose or issue to discuss, bring by an article that you think may be of interest to a person, or ask for advice in an area in which the individual has particular expertise. Again, it doesn't have to be work related. You can ask for a referral to a good pediatrician from someone who has children, or for a recommendation for a Friday-night movie.

• *Spiritual or religious groups.* Aside from recommending volunteer work, your church, synagogue, or other spiritual meeting place might have groups that you can join. Frequently, these organizations have groups tailored for various segments of the community—for single parents, singles in search of friendship, and the like—and typically welcome all prospective members.

For some people, it may be helpful to view networking the way you view physical exercise: it may be difficult (and sometimes painful), but you know it's good for you. Just as you wouldn't begin a running regimen with a twenty-six-mile marathon, don't choose the hardest opportunity you can think of as your first networking activity. It will only turn you off and make you reluctant to do it over the long term. How you network, or what groups you choose to join, isn't nearly as important as just getting out there, meeting people, and having a good time at it.

S trategies for Internal Networking

1. Organize group outings (but take care not to be viewed as a "camp counselor").
2. Join a task force.
3. Introduce people to one another.
4. Remember names and personal information.
5. Circulate articles to others who have similar interests or needs.
6. Reach out for help when you need it.
7. Mentor newcomers to your field.
8. Invite colleagues and their families to your home for a barbecue or potluck.
9. Keep a list of people with special talents to whom you can refer others.
10. Bring together people with similar interests over lunch or dinner.

S trategies for External Networking

11. Volunteer for a nonprofit board or committee.
12. Be an active member of a professional organization.
13. Stay in touch at the holidays with people you may not see throughout the year.
14. Take up a sport that requires at least one other person to participate and make time to play regularly.
15. Join a service or community organization (e.g., Rotary, Kiwanis, Lions, chamber of commerce).
16. Be active in your college or university's alumni association.
17. Join a motivational group, such as LEADS or The Breakfast Club.
18. Be a docent at your local museum.
19. Do volunteer work for a political party.
20. Join a "fun" club (e.g., Sierra Club, a book club, a restaurant club).
21. Conduct pro bono workshops in your area of expertise for nonprofit organizations.
22. Attend public meetings on community issues.
23. Carry plenty of business cards.
24. Write articles for professional journals.

Resources

Now that you understand why successful people derail, and ways in which you may be teetering on the brink of it yourself, it is time to make a commitment to do something to prevent it. The following quotation from Johann Wolfgang von Goethe, one of the greatest and most versatile European writers and thinkers of modern times, sums up the need to take affirmative action on behalf of your career success:

> *Until one is committed, there is hesitancy, the chance to draw back, always ineffectiveness. Concerning all acts of initiative (and creation), there is one elementary truth, the ignorance of which kills countless ideas and splendid plans: that the moment one definitely commits oneself, then providence moves too.*
>
> *All sorts of things occur to help one that would never otherwise have occurred. A whole stream of events issues from the decision, raising in one's favor all manner of unforeseen incidents and*

*meetings and material assistance, which no one could have
dreamed would have come their way.*

Whatever you do, or dream you can, begin it.

Boldness has genius, power and magic in it.

Begin it now.

In addition to the suggestions provided at the end of each
chapter (including, hopefully, a few of your own) I've also made
references to classes, programs, and reading materials throughout
the book that might assist you with developing a plan for overcoming your strengths. Herein you will find a comprehensive list-
ing of resources that you can call on to help you develop skills in
a particular area. They are divided by the type of resource (books,
consultants, training programs, etc.) and include phone numbers,
addresses, and other references.

Do not misconstrue this list as one of products or services that
I endorse without qualification. Don't assume that other resources
not included are without value. Although I have taken care to include only consultants, companies, and products of which I have
firsthand knowledge, your selection of any person or item included in this chapter should be made only after your own careful
research and consideration. Consult with your personnel or human
resources department for help with identifying alternative resources in your area.

Professional and Executive Coaches

The philosophies, styles, and fees of coaches vary greatly. Because
after the initial face-to-face coaching session much of the remaining work is done over the telephone, the geographic location of a
coach is not always the best determinant for selection. The most
important considerations in selecting any coach are:

1. Assuring that there is a match between your personality and the coach's personality;
2. Assessing the coach's expertise in the area in which you require assistance (e.g., presentation skills, interpersonal skills, career development); and
3. Locating a coach whose fee fits within your budget. (Many companies today will pay for employee coaching in much the same way as they pay for other training programs. Check with your human resources department.)

When it comes to selecting a coach, be a smart consumer. Especially if your company is paying for it, you may get only one chance to be coached, so don't settle for someone with whom you have never spoken. So much of successful coaching depends on the coach-client relationship. Ask to speak with the coach in advance, either by phone or in a personal meeting, and ask questions such as:

- What is your coaching philosophy?
- What companies have sent clients to you for coaching?
- Are there any kinds of clients you don't like working with?
- How much time will be spent in face-to-face contact versus phone contact?
- What kind of information will you share with my employer?
- How long will the coaching process last?
- What kind of follow-up with you can I expect?
- Will you provide me with a written action plan?
- Do you make referrals to other professionals when needed?

Whether the coach you select is across the street from your office or across the country, you can anticipate that the coaching process will more or less follow these steps:

Phase 1. There will be a discussion that allows you and the coach to become acquainted and determine logistics. If you live at a significant distance from the coach's office, this initial discussion may take place by phone.

Phase 2. The coach will solicit feedback about your performance from colleagues, management, and, when applicable, staff reporting to you. This will be done through either interviews, the use of a feedback instrument, or both. Again, depending on distance, interviews may be conducted in person or by phone.

Phase 3. What follows is one or more days of in-depth, face-to-face discussions with the coach (you may go to the coach's office, or he or she to yours). If your offices are near one another, these sessions may be more frequent but of shorter duration.

Phase 4. Ongoing telephone consultation and follow-up sessions can be expected for anywhere from three months to a year.

Business has seen a proliferation of coaches over the past several years, each with their own unique niches. Here are the names of several whom I know to be professional and reputable:

J. DOUGLAS ANDREWS, PH.D.
THE UNIVERSITY OF SOUTHERN CALIFORNIA
SCHOOL OF BUSINESS ADMINISTRATION, ACC 400
LOS ANGELES, CA 90089-1421
213-740-5959

Dr. Doug Andrews, assistant dean and chair of USC's Department of Business Communication, works with executives in developing their communication skills. He incorporates his twenty-five years of corporate and academic experience into a perspective that helps executives develop and articulate their goals and objectives in environments that are being constantly reengineered.

COMMUNICATION DEVELOPMENT ASSOCIATES, INC.
21550 OXNARD STREET, SUITE 880
WOODLAND HILLS, CA 91367
818-587-9000

Founded in 1976, Communication Development Associates (CDA) provides communication consultation and coaching to executives and professionals around the world. At the heart of its work is a sharp focus on providing practical suggestions and insights about communication effectiveness. CDA serves its client base in both individual and group settings, specializing in improving one-to-one interactions, meeting communication, and stand-up presentation skills.

CORPORATE COACHING INTERNATIONAL
445 SOUTH FIGUEROA STREET, SUITE 2700
LOS ANGELES, CA 90071
800-544-1177

The philosophy of Corporate Coaching International (CCI) is that in order for coaching to be effective it must take into consideration the career, interpersonal, and psychosocial aspects of individual development. CCI's staff includes experts in all three areas and, depending on the issues being addressed, you may be coached by one or more of the firm's associates. CCI offers different levels of coaching services for professionals, managers, and executives, each designed to fit the client's time and financial considerations.

NANCY HUTCHENS & ASSOCIATES, INC.
ORGANIZATIONAL CONSULTING
329 SPRING STREET
OSSINING, NY 10562
914-762-8392

Dr. Nancy Hutchens is a business skills coach who has a track record of helping motivated managers and professionals become more effective. Her coaching approach incorporates three basic requirements for individual change: 360° feedback about how others perceive one's behavior; an understanding of performance expectations and management priorities; and support from one's management or team leader critical to the final outcome. Dr. Hutchens facilitates discussion between clients and managers to ensure there is consensus about the issues and solutions.

DENNIS PERKINS, PH.D.
250 WEST MAIN STREET
BRANFORD, CT 06405
203-481-6118
FAX: 203-481-5531

Dr. Perkins's approach places work in the context of a balanced life structure, emphasizing the importance of both physical and psychological well-being. He specializes in working with highly creative individuals who are having difficulty realizing their full potential and capitalizing on their unique personal qualities. In addition to his coaching work, Dr. Perkins also acts as a consultant to senior managers on leadership and strategic change.

PHOENIX CONSULTANTS
5627 ARCHCREST DRIVE
LOS ANGELES, CA 90043
213-294-5648

Phoenix Human Resources is a full-service training and development firm that specializes in helping women and people of color to redirect and renew their careers. Recognizing that this particular population has career and performance challenges that are typically not addressed using mainstream techniques, Phoenix helps companies and employees to assure that differences are valued and utilized. Based on the premise that coaching is effective only when both the company and the individual see value in remaining with the career or organization, Phoenix tailors its efforts to meet the specific needs of both.

SUSAN PICASCIA, MSW
11712 MOORPARK, SUITE 207
STUDIO CITY, CA 91604
818-752-1787

Susan Picascia, MSW, combines her experience in the fields of mental health and human resources to help maximize individual growth directed toward achievement of corporate goals. Assessing job-person fit; the emotional, psychological, and spiritual aspects of personal development; and corporate culture are key to her coaching philosophy. She integrates management and employee coaching techniques to assure a balanced approach to conflict resolution.

Companies Offering Public Workshops or Training Programs

There are numerous companies that offer public (as opposed to customized in-house) workshops on a variety of topics. Programs are typically held several times throughout the year in various cities across the country. Included here are several companies that cover a wide range of developmental areas. I recommend that you write or phone each company to request a course catalog that lists all of their programs along with the content, location, and cost for each program.

AMERICAN MANAGEMENT ASSOCIATION
135 WEST 50TH STREET
NEW YORK, NY 10020
800-262-9699

The American Management Association (AMA) offers more than two hundred seminars for employees at all levels within an organization. Their programs typically provide participants with hands-on techniques for increasing effectiveness in areas such as communication skills, strategic management, assertiveness, management skills, and accounting. Here is a sampling of their course titles:

FUNDAMENTALS OF FINANCE AND ACCOUNTING FOR NONFINANCIAL EXECUTIVES

MANAGEMENT SKILLS AND TECHNIQUES FOR NEW SUPERVISORS

BUSINESS PRINCIPLES FOR THE EXECUTIVE ASSISTANT

STRATEGY IMPLEMENTATION

LISTEN UP! A STRATEGIC APPROACH TO BETTER LISTENING

NEGOTIATING TO WIN

AMA also has a self-study catalog that can be requested by phoning 800-225-3215.

THE CENTER FOR CREATIVE LEADERSHIP
P.O. BOX 26300
GREENSBORO, NC 27438-6300
919-288-7210

The Center for Creative Leadership (CCL) is a nonprofit educational institute with branches throughout the country and in Europe. It works to adapt the theories and ideas of the behavioral sciences to the practical concerns of managers and leaders throughout society. Through research, training, and publication CCL addresses the challenges facing leaders of today and tomorrow. They offer outstanding programs for executives and senior managers as well as an array of publications related to leadership.

DALE CARNEGIE
INTERNATIONAL HEADQUARTERS
1475 FRANKLIN AVENUE
GARDEN CITY, NY 11530
516-248-5100
FAX: 516-248-5817

Many of us remember Dale Carnegie's former slogan: "how to win friends and influence people." The Dale Carnegie Course, offered at various locations around the world, is designed to provide you with the skills and confidence needed to communicate effectively, deal with problem solving, and inspire coworkers. Course objectives include developing more self-confidence, controlling your fear of an audience, improving your memory, developing a more effective personality, and widening your personal horizons. Additionally, they offer both college credit and continuing education credits (CEUs) to anyone participating in their programs.

NTL INSTITUTE
1240 N. PITT STREET, SUITE 100
ALEXANDRIA, VA 22314
800-777-5227
703-548-1500

NTL, founded in 1947, offers an array of workshops for those who want to develop their interpersonal skills. Their workshops are experientially oriented and provide participants with the opportunity to explore their own values, attitudes, and actions as well as how others perceive them. They create a positive and supportive environment in which participants are free to explore behavior changes. A sampling of NTL's workshops include:

THE HUMAN INTERACTION LABORATORY asks participants to assess their behaviors and interpersonal styles in relation to others and learn how to give and receive feedback effectively, project a more positive presence, and gain insight into their true potential.

POWER: HOW TO CREATE IT, KEEP IT, AND USE IT EFFECTIVELY is for anyone who wants to discover and develop sources of personal power and learn how to influence others effectively; investigate ways to focus intellectual, emotional, and physical power; and identify self-imposed limits to power and explore ways to overcome them.

LEADERSHIP EXCELLENCE is an advanced workshop for middle and upper-middle managers who want to improve their skills in leading and working with others. It focuses on building and maintaining high-performing organizations.

I have attended a number of NTL workshops and recommend them highly. A client who attended one of their programs described it as "a life-changing experience." Be aware that because they are experientially oriented, they can be quite intense and require more than simply passive participation.

OUTWARD BOUND
NATIONAL OFFICE
ROUTE 9D, R2 BOX 280
GARRISON, NY 10524-9757
800-243-8520
914-424-4000

Outward Bound courses are designed to help people develop self-confidence, compassion, and an appreciation for selfless service to others. They are not a survival school. Their challenging curriculum enables participants to learn by doing, and personal growth is central to the Outward Bound experience. Their programs enable you to realize individual success and encourage you to develop a team spirit that results in the camaraderie and interdependence necessary for your team to achieve its goals. In addition to their public programs, they also customize events for individual company retreats or team buildings. I highly recommend an Outward Bound program for anyone who wants to learn to take more risks, develop confidence, and understand the value of teamwork.

TOASTMASTER'S INTERNATIONAL

WORLD HEADQUARTERS

23182 ARROYO VISTA

RANCHO SANTA MARGARITA, CA 92688

800-993-7732

714-858-8255

Toastmaster's is not really a workshop, but rather a group of businesspeople who meet regularly to discuss and practice issues related to presentation skills. There are chapters located throughout the world, most typically in downtown business districts. You can use the toll-free number above to find out where groups meet in your area. People who belong to Toastmaster's report a significant increase in their comfort level and skill in speaking before groups. Even if you don't have occasion to do a lot of public speaking, participation can help you to improve your verbal communication.

Classes

You'll need to do some legwork to find classes, degree programs, and groups that will address your specific developmental needs. These kinds of learning experiences can be more beneficial than a workshop because they provide the opportunity to explore a topic in greater depth and, typically, provide time to practice or apply the skill. Most major cities have universities and community colleges that offer programs through extension schools that are targeted for the working person. Some public television stations even offer classes.

These are a few classes that I recommend that you consider:

ACTING. People are often surprised when I recommend an acting class as part of their developmental plans. Acting classes can help you to overcome discomfort in front of groups, allow your emotions to emerge, and hone your presentation style. They require that you pay more attention to the fact that we are all actors on a corporate stage.

ART. Art classes are great for bringing out your creative talents—something you can later apply to strategic thinking. Even if you don't consider yourself an artist, take a drawing, sculpting, or painting class and allow yourself to use the side of your brain that may not normally be put to use.

ASSERTIVENESS. I prefer that assertiveness be learned through a class rather than at a one-day workshop, because this skill requires practice over time. A class allows you to practice the techniques taught one week, and return the next week to fine-tune them.

CREATIVE WRITING. In addition to the fact that a writing class can stimulate creative thinking, it can help you to hone your business writing skills.

DRAWING. A beginning course in drawing can help to develop and expand your observational abilities.

INNER CHILD. They may be called by different names, but inner-child programs are designed to enable participants to work through childhood issues that continue to influence present life functioning.

JOURNAL WRITING. Especially when used in conjunction with coaching, psychotherapy, or other workshops, keeping a journal can be a valuable tool to help you clarify your thoughts, feelings, goals, and objectives.

PHOTOGRAPHY. A photography class can help you to look at the world differently and, when combined with learning to use the darkroom, can assist you with paying closer attention to detail.

SELF-DEFENSE. As well as providing skill in the obvious, self-defense classes can also be particularly useful in developing assertiveness and increased self-esteem.

TIME MANAGEMENT. A time-management class is especially appropriate for anyone who finds himself or herself saying that there is no time to develop skill in the areas included in this book! It can help you to take back control of your work environment so that you have more time to focus on matters pertaining to your own career development.

YOGA. Taking a yoga class may seem a bit far out to many businesspeople, but in reality it can have a number of beneficial effects. Through meditation and exercise it can help to diminish stress, increase focus, and enhance clarity of thought. Some of what you learn in a yoga class can even be practiced in the privacy of your office.

Inventories and Self-Assessment Tools

No inventory or test can tell you more about yourself than you already know. They can, however, help you to understand your own behaviors and ways in which to maximize your natural talents. When it comes to using a 360° feedback instrument, a tool through which colleagues give you feedback as to how they perceive you, results can be surprising and difficult to comprehend. Therefore, use such tools carefully and, whenever possible, in conjunction with professional guidance. Such guidance can come in the form of a coach, mentor, human resources professional, or psychologist.

BEHAVIORAL SCIENCE RESOURCES
P.O. BOX 411
PROVO, UT 84603-0411
801-375-9600

I recommend using Behavioral Science Resources (BSR) for purchasing and processing feedback instruments. BSR pioneered the use of survey feedback—now commonly known as 360° feedback. The company's instruments are designed to collect the perceptions and comments of all work associates and specific instruments are geared toward collecting feedback relevant to professional, supervisory, and management behaviors. Feedback profiles can be used for individual coaching, team building, peer review, and training needs assessment. BSR also sponsors a seminar for in-depth individual assessment or trainer "certification."

CONSULTING PSYCHOLOGISTS PRESS, INC.
3803 E. BAYSHORE ROAD
PALO ALTO, CA 94303
800-624-1765
415-969-8901

Consulting Psychologists Press (CPP) is the publisher of the Myers Briggs Type Indicator and other self-assessment tools. CPP's business catalog includes assessment instruments and reference materials useful in organization, career, leadership, and management development. Not all of their psychological instruments are available to the general public, so ask your human resources department for assistance when specialized skills or education are required.

PFEIFFER & COMPANY
2780 CIRCLEPORT DRIVE
ERLANGER, KY 41018
800-274-4434

Known primarily as a resource for trainers and consultants, Pfeiffer offers a comprehensive array of tools, instruments, and reference materials for developing individuals and teams. Although many of the offerings contained in the company's catalog will be of interest to only human resources professionals, the layperson will find items such as the Leadership Development Inventory, *The Team Handbook, Group Power: The Manager's Guide to Using Task Force Meetings,* and *Career Anchors,* to name a few, useful in personal development.

Teleometrics International
1755 Woodstead Court
The Woodlands, TX 77380
800-527-0406

Teleometrics produces videos and publishes self-assessment tools on topics such as empowerment, motivation, interpersonal relations, organizational culture, and conflict and change. Not only are the company's instruments validated, reliable, and research based, but they also include clear and understandable instructions for interpretation.

Books

Books about how to succeed in business by really trying (or not really trying) are abundant. All you need to do to find them is to visit your local bookstore and peruse the career, self-help, business, or management aisles. In an effort to help you select ones that might be most useful, a reference is included for each of the books mentioned throughout the previous chapters and a few additional ones that are worth taking a look at.

The Artist's Way: A Spiritual Path to Higher Creativity
Julia Cameron with Mark Bryan, G. P. Putnam's Sons, 1992

*Beware the Naked Man Who Offers You His Shirt: Do What You
Love, Love What You Do, and Deliver More Than You Promise*
Harvey MacKay, Ballantine Books, 1990

Certain Trumpets: The Call of Leaders
Garry Wills, Simon & Schuster, 1994

Coping with an Intolerable Boss
Michael M. Lombardo and Morgan W. McCall Jr., Center for
    Creative Leadership, 1984
(You'll have to call CCL at the number listed above to obtain a
copy of this monograph.)

Danger in the Comfort Zone
Judith M. Bardwick, AMACOM, 1991

*Drawing on the Right Side of the Brain: A Course in Enhancing
Creativity and Artistic Confidence*
Betty Edwards, J. P. Tarcher, 1979

Emotional Intelligence
Daniel Goleman, Bantam Books, 1995

Encyclopedia of Associations
Updated annually and available through Gale Research at 800-
877-GALE, or check with your local library.

*Finding Your Perfect Work: The New Career Guide to Making a
Living, Creating a Life*
Paul and Sarah Edwards, Putnam, 1996

Gifts Differing
Isabel Briggs Myers with Peter B. Myers, Consulting Psycholo-
    gists Press, Inc., 1980

Hardball for Women: Winning at the Game of Business
Pat Heim, Ph.D., with Susan K. Golant, Plume, 1993

Influencing with Integrity: Management Skills for Communication and Negotiation
Genie Z. Laborde, Syntony Publishing, 1987
(Don't be thrown by the title. It's not only for managers—everyone can learn influence skills from this one.)

Letitia Baldrige's New Complete Guide to Executive Manners
Letitia Baldrige, Rawson Associates, 1993

The Magic of Conflict
Thomas F. Crum, Touchstone/Simon & Schuster, 1987

Mining Group Gold: How to Cash In on the Collaborative Power of a Group
Thomas A. Kayser, Serif Publishing, 1990

Paradigms: The Business of Discovering the Future
Joel Arthur Barker, HarperBusiness, 1992

People Skills: How to Assert Yourself, Listen to Others, and Resolve Conflicts
Robert Bolton, Ph.D., Simon & Schuster, 1979

The Plateauing Trap
Judith Bardwick, Ph.D., Bantam Books, 1986

Please Understand Me: Character & Temperament Types
David Kiersey and Marilyn Bates, Gnosology Books, 1984
(If you aren't qualified to purchase the Myers Briggs Type Indicator, this book contains a variation of it with a complete explanation of your score and type preferences.)

Preventing Derailment: What to Do Before It's Too Late
Michael M. Lombardo and Robert W. Eichinger, Center for Creative Leadership, 1987
(You'll have to call CCL at the number listed above to obtain a copy of this monograph.)

Sacred Hoops: Spiritual Lessons of a Hardwood Warrior
Phil Jackson and Hugh Delehanty, Hyperion, 1995

Servant Leadership: A Journey into the Nature of Legitimate Power and Greatness
Robert K. Greenleaf, Paulist Press, 1977

Talking from 9 to 5: How Women's and Men's Conversational Styles Affect Who Gets Heard, Who Gets Credit, and What Gets Done at Work
Deborah Tannen, Ph.D., William Morrow and Company, 1994

Taming Your Gremlin: A Guide to Enjoying Yourself
Richard D. Carson, HarperPerennial, 1983

The Tao of Leadership: Leadership Strategies for a New Age
John Heider, Bantam New Age Books, 1988

Team Players and Teamwork
Glenn M. Parker, Jossey-Bass, 1996

Type Talk at Work: How the 16 Personality Types Determine Your Success on the Job
Otto Kroeger with Janet M. Thuesen, Tilden Press, 1992

The Way of the Wizard: 20 Lessons for Living a Magical Life
Deepak Chopra, Crown Publishers, 1995

What Color Is Your Parachute: A Practical Manual for Job Hunters & Career Changers
Richard N. Bolles, Ten Speed Press, 1995

When Money Is Not Enough: Fulfillment in Work
Eileen R. Hannegan, M.S., Beyond Words Publishing, 1995

The Wisdom of Teams: Creating the High Performance Organization
Jon R. Katzenbach and Douglas K. Smith, Harvard Business
School Press, 1993

Women, Anger, and Depression: Strategies for Self-Empowerment
Lois P. Frankel, Ph.D., Health Communications, 1991

*You Just Don't Understand: Women and Men
in Conversation*
Deborah Tannen, Ph.D., Ballantine Books, 1990

*Zen and the Art of Making a Living: A Practical Guide to Creative
Career Design*
Lawrence G. Boldt, Penguin, 1993

Magazines and Newspapers

In addition to subscribing to and reading technical journals related to your field, it is also important that you have a breadth,
if not depth, of knowledge of current affairs, business events,
and issues relating to the workplace. For this reason, I am including a wide variety of magazines that will help to keep you
abreast of all three—and stretch you to explore issues that you
might not normally. For example, if you have a difficult time
making small talk in conversation, try reading *Sports Illustrated*
or *People* magazine so that you have an idea of what's going on in
the world of sports or entertainment and can refer to something
interesting that you've read. My suggestion is that you subscribe
to and make time to read at least three of the following on a regular basis:

TIME	HARPER'S	SPORTS ILLUSTRATED
HARVARD BUSINESS REVIEW	PEOPLE NEWSWEEK WORKING WOMAN	NEW YORK TIMES CONDÉ NAST TRAVELER
WALL STREET JOURNAL THE NEW YORKER	SCIENCE OMNI	YOUR LOCAL NEWSPAPER
READER'S DIGEST	WORTH FORTUNE	MS.

Mental Health Contacts

If you think that the help that you require goes beyond the scope of a workshop, coach, or book, you might want to consider entering into counseling with a licensed mental health practitioner. Most business coaches report that about 75 percent of the people they coach are referred for some kind of longer-term counseling in conjunction with or following the coaching. Counseling isn't for people who are "sick," but rather for people who want to lead fuller, more productive lives. Good counseling can help you to understand what part your past plays in the present and how to avoid allowing it to control your life.

Most people will do well with a licensed psychologist or psychotherapist. Psychiatrists are physicians (M.D.'s) who typically use a medical model for the treatment of psychological problems. Psychiatrists can prescribe drugs whereas the other two classifications cannot. I recommend beginning with a psychologist or psychotherapist and, if needed, a referral can then be made to a psychiatrist.

There are many people who call themselves counselors or psychotherapists, and licensing varies from state to state. When seeking psychological assistance you want to evaluate a number of things: the person's professional credentials and licenses, his or her experience dealing with the problems you want to address, the match between you and the therapist, and the cost. Don't be afraid to ask questions. Remember, you are the consumer.

Depending on the part of the country in which you live, the average cost of therapy can range anywhere from $75 per hour to $150 per hour or more. When you are ready to find a therapist, there are a number of ways to locate someone reputable.

1. **REFERRAL FROM A TRUSTED FRIEND OR RELATIVE.** This is probably the best way to find a therapist. Be aware, however, that just because your best friend loves his or her therapist, it doesn't mean you will too. Give yourself at least three or four sessions before you decide a particular therapist isn't for you.

2. **YOUR FAMILY PHYSICIAN.** Your own physician can be a good source for a referral. Make certain that you let him or her know what you are looking for in a therapist so that an appropriate referral can be made.

3. **LOCAL MENTAL HEALTH AGENCIES.** If you look in the yellow pages under "mental health" there are agencies listed that provide psychological services. These are often nonprofit community agencies where treatment is reasonably priced.

4. **YOUR COMPANY'S EMPLOYEE ASSISTANCE PROGRAM (EAP).** Many companies today have EAPs that are designed to help employees in distress. Some even offer a limited number of confidential therapy sessions paid for by the company. Ask your personnel or human resources manager for more information.

5. **THE AMERICAN PSYCHOLOGICAL ASSOCIATION (APA).** APA consists of members who are licensed psychologists and psychotherapists. Each state has a chapter of the APA and can refer you to a licensed member in your area. When calling information

ask for the name of your state's Psychological Association (e.g., Illinois Psychological Association).

You can avoid derailment by following the suggestions given herein and taking advantage of one or more of these resources. Remember, your career lies not in the hands of your boss or management, but in the choices you make next. You have no control over the past, but you can take charge of your future. Begin today to overcome your strengths.

Index

About the Author

LOIS P. FRANKEL, Ph.D., cofounder of the Los Angeles–based firm The Frankel & Fox Group, Consultants in Employee Development, has nearly twenty years' experience in the field of human resources development. She travels internationally to consult with organizations of all sizes to help them meet their business objectives by maximizing the development of individuals and teams. With particular expertise in coaching individuals to reach their full career potential, she also designs and facilitates training programs related to achieving superior team performance, leadership development, and the empowerment of women in the workplace.

Dr. Frankel is the author of numerous employment-related journal articles as well as two previous books: *Kindling the Spirit: Acts of Kindness and Words of Courage for Women* and *Women, Anger, and Depression: Strategies for Self-Empowerment* (Health Communications). A member of the Society for Human Resources Management, the American Psychological Association, and the Organization Development Network, she is a licensed psychotherapist with a doctorate in counseling psychology from the University of Southern California.